COPYRIGHT

interpreting the law
for libraries and archives

COPYRIGHT

interpreting the law
for libraries and archives

Graham P. Cornish

Copyright Officer
British Library

THE LIBRARY ASSOCIATION

LONDON

© The Library Association 1990

Published by
Library Association Publishing Ltd
7 Ridgmount Street
London WC1E 7AE

First published 1990

British Library Cataloguing in Publication Data

Cornish, G. P. (Graham Peter)
  Copyright : interpreting the law for libraries and archives.
  1. Great Britain. Copyright. Law
  I. Title
  344.106482

ISBN 0-85365-709-2

Typeset in 10/12pt Times by Library Association Publishing Ltd
Printed and made in Great Britain by Bookcraft (Bath) Ltd

Contents

List of abbreviations

AACR2	Anglo-American Cataloguing Rules Second Edition
BLAISE	British Library Automated Information Service
BNB	British National Bibliography
CCC	Copyright Clearance Center
CD-ROM	Compact Disc—Read Only Memory
CLA	Copyright Licensing Agency
HMSO	Her Majesty's Stationery Office
NHS	National Health Service
OCLC	Online Computer Library Center
OCR	Optical Character Recognition
OHP	Overhead Projector
PC	Personal Computer
PLR	Public Lending Right
SDI	Selective Dissemination of Information
SI	Statutory Instruments
USGPO	United States Government Printing Office
VAT	Value Added Tax
UCC	Universal Copyright Convention

Author's note

This book tries to set out the basics of the new copyright law, concentrating on those areas which may affect librarians and archivists in their daily work. There are many areas which have not been dealt with at all such a public performance, and aspects of broadcasting and publishing, while the whole area of design and patents is left to others far more competent to deal with them in those areas where they impinge on the work of libraries.

The book is organized on a question and answer pattern to simplify searching for particular problems and their possible solutions. Because of this there is a small amount of repetition between sections. This is quite deliberate to avoid unnecessary 'see also' comments which tend to confuse or bewilder the user. Obviously not every possible question can be answered but every effort has been made to anticipate those which arise most often. The law is not there to deal in specific terms with any and every possible situation but to provide the framework within which decisions can be made in specific circumstances. There are always 'grey' areas of interpretation or circumstance when the law will be unclear. Where this is obviously the case, the book tries to offer guidance rather than provide a definite answer as this is just not always possible. It should be remembered that what the law does not allow can often be done with the copyright owner's consent through an appropriate licence. Therefore, where the book says that the law prevents something, librarians and archivists should first check to see what kind of licence, if any, their institution holds for copying beyond the stated limits. In a book of this kind it is not possible to say what existing licences allow as they will differ between different kinds of institution and will change with time.

The author has been advising the British Library Document Supply centre on copyright matters for several years and took part in many of the discussions which helped to shape the library profession's reaction to the new legislation. He served (and serves) on a number of working groups and committees dealing with copyright matters and has lectured and run seminars on copyright law both in the UK and abroad. The wealth of information and opinion gathered from these contacts has been used to compile this book but it must be remembered it is written by a librarian trying to understand the law, not a lawyer trying to understand libraries!

Graham P. Cornish
British Library Document Supply Centre
Boston Spa
December 1989

Introduction

The idea behind copyright is rooted in certain fundamental ideas about creativity and possession. Basially, it springs from the idea that anything we create is an extension of 'self' and should be protected from general use by anyone else. Coupled with this is the idea that the person creating something has exclusive rights over the thing created, partly for economic reasons but also because of this extension of 'self' idea. Copyright is therefore important to ensure the continued growth of writing, performing and creating. Copyright law aims to protect this growth but, at the same time, tries to ensure that some access to copyright works is allowed as well. Without this access creators would be starved of ideas and information to create more copyright material.

Libraries are in a unique position as custodians of copyright material. They have the duty to care for, and allow access to, other people's copyright works. This places special responsibilities on all those working in libraries, archives and the information world generally. We practise our profession by using this property so we should take all possible steps to protect it, whilst, at the same time, ensuring that the rights and privileges of our users are also safeguarded.

Because copyright is such an intangible thing, there is often a temptation to ignore it. Those who take this approach forget that they, too, own copyright in their own creations and would feel quite angry if this were abused by others. Some of the restrictions placed on use by the law may seem petty or trivial but they are designed to allow some use of copyright material without unduly harming the interests of the creator (author).

The new Copyright Act differs substantially from the one of 1956, and anyone familiar with the old Act should not make any assumptions as to the content of the new one. Many definitions have changed, new rights have been introduced, library copying has been linked to fair dealing and licensing as a concept is firmly established by the Act.

The introduction of new legislation often has the effect of heightening awareness of the subject, making people more keen to know their rights and privileges and generally creating an atmosphere of extreme caution in case anyone puts a foot wrong and ends up in court. Although this is a good thing, nobody should become too paranoid. Most infringements of copyright are dealt with through the civil courts so that the rights owner must take legal proceedings if it is thought an infringement has taken place.

The Act also sets the stage for a completely new approach to the use of copyright material. Now that we all know what the law says (even if we do not always know what it means!) there is scope to develop services outside the allowances which the Copyright Act makes by talking to the licensing agencies and other rights' owners' organizations to negotiate use of material in return for royalties. Those working in the information industries should not lose sight of this as a real way forward when the law inhibits the introduction of new services without the owners' consent. Licences granted by copyright owners can also override the limitations set by the law.

SECTION ONE

Definition and law

1. Q. What is copyright?
   A. Copyright is a property right intended to protect the rights of those who create works of various kinds. The protection is to prevent exploitation of their works by others. It follows that copyright cannot exist by itself but only within the work which has been created. For this reason we say that copyright 'subsists' rather than exists.

2. Q. What is the latest legislation?
   A. The Copyright, Designs and Patents Act, 1988 which came into force on 1 August 1989, and the supporting Regulations. There are a number of these but the Statutory Instruments which affect libraries and archives most are:

   SI 89/816 Copyright Designs and Patents Act 1988 (Commencement No.1) Order
   SI 89/1012. Copyright (Recordings of Folksongs for Archives) (Designated Bodies) Order
   SI 89/1067 Copyright (Application of Provisions relating to Educational Establishments to Teachers) (No.2) Order
   SI 89/1068 Copyright (Educational Establishments) (No.2) Order
   SI 89/1098. The Copyright (Material Open to Public Inspection) (International Organizations) Order
   SI 89/1099. The Copyright (Material Open to Public Inspection) (Making of Copies of Maps) Order
   SI 89/1212. Copyright (Librarians and Archivists) (Copying of Copyright Materials) Order
   SI 89/1293. Copyright (Application to Other Countries) (No.2) Order
   SI 90/2510 The Copyright (Recording for Archives of

1

Designated Class of Broadcasts and Cable Programmes)
(Designated Bodies)(No.2) Order

It is important to note that a number of defective Statutory
Instruments were drawn up for this Act and never imple-
mented. The above list includes all those of direct relevance
to libraries and archives. Other SIs with the same title but
different numbering were replaced by those listed and the
earlier ones should be ignored.

SECTION TWO

What is covered

---

3. Q. What things are covered by copyright?
    A. Virtually anything that is printed, written, recorded in any form, or anything that can be made by a human being. The law divides these items into various classes and all aspects of them are dealt with separately in the following pages.

4. Q. Does absolutely anything in these groups qualify for copyright?
    A. No, not quite. Works first published in, or by nationals of, certain countries are not protected (see question 8). Also the work has to be original.

4a. Q. What does 'original' mean?
    A. The law does not say, but the idea is that to be protected the author must have contributed quite a lot of his or her own ideas or skills to the making of the work.
    Example. If you write your own poem about Jack and Jill, it is protected. If you simply reproduce the well-known nursery rhyme with one or two minor changes, that is not original and not protected (but the typographical arrangement may be, see questions 274-282)

5. Q. Is the title of a book or journal article protected by copyright?
    A. Rarely. Such titles are statements of fact—they tell you what the book or article is called—and cannot therefore be protected unless they are so complex that they become a literary work in their own right or are registered as a trademark.

6. Q. Is there copyright in facts?
    A. No. A fact is a fact and cannot be protected as such. However, the way in which information about facts is presented is protected.
    Example. Times of trains are facts and nobody can prevent

3

you from publishing information that trains leave at certain times for particular places. What is protected is (*a*) the layout of the timetable and (*b*) the actual typography. So you might make this information available by including it in a brochure about a tourist attraction but it would be an infringement to photocopy the timetable and reprint this in the brochure.

7. Q. What are the qualifications necessary to claim copyright?
    A. The person claiming to be the author must be a UK citizen or a citizen of a country where UK works are protected in the same way as in Britain (see question 8). A complete list of these countries is given in SI 89/1293. Also anyone carrying out work for the Crown, Parliament, the United Nations or the Organization of American States has that work protected as if it were published in the UK, even if the author is a national of a country not otherwise covered by these arrangements. See also Questions 410-414.

8. Q. Are any works excepted from the usual copyright protection?
    A. Yes. The Bible, the Book of Common Prayer of the Church of England and Sir James Barrie's *Peter Pan*. All enjoy special protection outside normal copyright limitations. The Authorized Version of the Bible and the Book of Common Prayer are printed under patents issued by the Crown and are therefore in perpetual copyright. This does not extend to modern versions which must be treated as published works which are anonymous, whatever one's personal theological view! The Bible and the Book of Common Prayer cannot be copied as they are outside copyright law. Permission is usually given for small quotations in published versions and photocopying of various portions for research or private study or reading in Church or chapel is not usually objected to. In the case of *Peter Pan*, the new Copyright Act has brought in perpetual copyright in this play for the benefit of the Hospital for Sick Children, Great Ormond Street, London. The Hospital owned the copyright which expired on 31 December 1987 and obtained a considerable revenue from it. Parliament decided to continue this privilege and any commercial publication or performance of the work attracts a royalty for the Hospital. This is a form of compulsory licensing for a work now out of copyright. As the Act did not come into force until 1 August 1989, any act of copying, commercial publication or per-

formance done between 31 December 1987 and 31 July 1989 was not an infringement. The play cannot be publicly performed without royalty payment to the Hospital for Sick Children.

9. Q. Is the whole and every little bit of a work protected?
    A. No. Copyright is limited by excluding from protection less than a substantial part of a work. So if less than a substantial part is copied there is no infringement except in certain areas.

10. Q. In which areas does this not apply?
    A. Mainly in educational establishments where copying for classroom use is limited by very strict amounts or the availability of a licence. See questions 121-131.

11. Q. What constitutes a substantial part?
    A. This is not defined. What is clear is that it is not just a question of quantity but quality as well.
        Example. Someone copies a page from a 250 page novel. It is unlikely that this one page is a substantial part of the whole work. Someone else copies the recommendations and conclusions (three paragraphs) from a 70-page technical report. This is almost certainly a substantial part. Similarly four bars of a symphony could constitute a substantial part because they encapsulate the theme music of the whole work.

12. Q. So are there any guidelines?
    A. Not really. Each case must be a matter of professional judgement. The British Copyright Council has issued a booklet giving some idea of what they considered not unreasonable but it is for guidance only. HMSO and Ordnance Survey also have special rules for which they issue guidelines.

SECTION THREE
Owner's rights

This section sets out what the owner is entitled to do exclusively in law. However, all rights also have limitations in order to exercise them, so the law limits these exclusive rights in a number of ways and this section should be interpreted in the light of what is said later about other people being allowed to do certain acts as well. It is these exceptions which form the bulk of this book.

13. Q. What rights does the law give the copyright owner?
    A. Copyright law gives the owner exclusive rights to do certain things to or with the copyright material. Nobody else is entitled to do these things.

14. Q. What are these owner's rights?
    A. There are five basic rights: (*a*) to copy the work; (*b*) to issue copies to the public; (*c*) to perform, show or play the work; (*d*) to broadcast the work; (*e*) to adapt the work. Each of these rights will be examined under the appropriate type of work.

15. Q. Are these absolute rights or do other people have some rights to use the material as well?
    A. They are not absolute because they are limited by (*a*) time; (*b*) quantity/quality; (*c*) purpose; and (*d*) certain exemptions given to user groups. Each of these limitations will be examined under the appropriate type of work.

SECTION FOUR

Literary, dramatic and musical works

These three classes are dealt with together because they are all treated in a similar way under the Copyright Act, although there are some differences in some specific areas.

Definitions

Literary works

16. Q. What is a literary work?
    A. The term 'literary work' includes anything that is printed or written such as books, journals, technical reports and manuscripts and also covers any works that are spoken or sung. It also includes tables (statistical, timetables, etc.) as well as computer programs and text stored electronically.
    Examples. The words of a popular song are protected as a literary work; the music is treated separately (see 'musical work' questions 23-25). The handwritten notes of an author are protected just as much as the final printed book. Railway timetables are protected as compilations although individual pieces of information within the timetable are not (see question 6).

17. Q. Does 'literary' mean it has to be good quality literature?
    A. No. Copyright law says almost nothing about the quality or content of the work. Literary means anything which is written, spoken or sung which has been recorded, whether in writing or some other way.
17a. Q. What about databases? Are these covered by copyright?
    A. This is not as simple as it might seem. The content of a database is protected as a literary work but the database *service* is protected differently. If a work is purely an in-house database created on a PC on an individual's desk or one such

7

as that created in a large company or local authority, then it is a literary work. If the database is one available to the public purely for viewing or for searching, such as BLAISE, then it becomes a cable programme and is not a literary work . However, if the database is the type where the user can add, delete or change information, like OCLC, then the database must be viewed as a literary work. The reason is that if signals can be sent between user and provider, other than for operating the system, then it is not a cable programme.

18. Q. Are bibliographic records covered by copyright?
    A. This is a difficult question and has never been clarified in law. The question is: is a bibliographic record 'Original'? Originality requires some intellectual input from the author. Most bibliographic records consist of a series of facts presented in a predetermined order according to AACR2 or other cataloguing codes of practice. In theory, everyone using these codes should produce exactly the same record. The fact that they do not is more to do with human fallibility than the rules themselves! Therefore it would be difficult to defend a catalogue record as having any copyright as such, although the typography in a published catalogue would be protected (see Question 21)

19. Q. So are bibliographies not protected by copyright?
    A. Yes, they are. They are certainly protected as compilations and cannot be copied beyond the substantial part allowed for any literary work.

20. Q. How much of a bibliography can be copied?
    A. It is impossible to answer with certainty. However, it would seem that a library could take a few records from, say, *BNB*, without infringing the copyright. But if the records for an entire class were taken, then this would be a substantial part and not justified. Similarly, to go through several years of *BNB* and take out all the reocrds from a particular class to make a bibliography would be an infringement.

21. Q. Could records be photocopied and put into a library catalogue?
    A. No. Athough each entry might well not attract copyright, there will certainly be copyright in the typography and by cutting it up and using the entries as catalogue cards this will infringe

8

the typographical arrangement as the use would not be for fair dealing.

(The term 'fair dealing' is crucial to understanding much of this book: see questions 97-120 for more detailed information.)

22. Q. Is a library catalogue protected?

A. It will depend on the form that it is kept in. If it is on cards, then each card could be protected, not so much as a catalogue record, but for its typographical arrangement. If it is on cards, then it will be unpublished and anonymous and therefore protected indefinitely until it is made available to the public. However, the real issue is the published library catalogue. This is protected for 50 years from the end of the year in which it is published as a compilation although individual entries will not be protected.

Dramatic works

23. Q. What is the difference between a literary and a dramatic work?

A. A dramatic work is the non-spoken part of a presentation and includes dance and mime. The words of a dramatic work are protected as a literary work.

Example. A show like *West Side Story*, will have separate copyrights in the words (literary work), the choreography and directions (dramatic work) and the music (musical work).

Musical works

24. Q. Does musical work mean anything with music included?

A. No. Musical work means only the music and excludes the words (which are a literary work) and any actions which go with the music because they are dramatic works.

Example. West Side Story (as mentioned above in 'dramatic works') will have three separate copyrights: (1) in the words; (2) in the actions and movements of the singers; (3) in the musical notes. Although this may sound complicated it is important because the people who composed the three elements will each own a separate copyright which may expire at different times. So the music might go out of copyright but not the words, or *vice versa*.

25. Q. Does musical work include a recording of the music?

A. No. That is separately covered as a sound recording.

25a. Q. What about a play performed and recorded on video?
    A. That is protected as a film quite separately.

Ownership of copyright

26. Q. Who owns the copyright in a work?
    A. Usually the author.

27. Q. Why only usually?
    A. Because the author may have assigned the copyright to someone else. It may have been sold to a publisher, given to someone else, left to someone in a will or automatically transferred to an employer. If the author created a work as part of his job, then his employer is usually the owner. However, there can be a contract between employer and employee which can state the opposite if required (i.e. the copyright remains with the employee). See the notes on commissioned works as well. There are special arrangements for Crown and Parliamentary Copyright (see questions 62-68). Also the author is differently defined for other classes of works such as films and sound recordings (see questions 333-334 and 372). For this reason most author's rights are referred to as owner's rights.

28. Q. Supposing the work was commissioned instead?
    A. If the work was commissioned after 1 August 1989, the copyright is owned by the author. Before that date it is usually the property of the person who paid for the commission.

29. Q. Supposing a library owns an original work such as a manuscript. Does the library own the copyright?
    A. Certainly not. it is important to distinguish between the object and the copyright which subsists in it. The library may own the manuscript but the copyright is still owned by the author or the person to whom it has been sold or assigned, so the library has no right to reproduce the manuscript, except as allowed by the Copyright Act.

30. Q. Who owns the copyright in a letter?
    A. The author, that is, the person who wrote the letter.

31. Q. Why does the person who received the letter not own it?
    A. Because copyright belongs to the person who creates the work.

10

The letter itself does belong to the person who received it. They were given it by the writer. But the copyright still belongs to the writer not the recipient of the letter.

Definition of author

32. Q. What is the definition of the author?
    A. The *person* who created the work.

33. Q. Supposing there are two or more authors?
    A. They all count as the authors of the copyright.

34. Q. Supposing it is not possible to find out who the author is?
    A. A work is considered anonymous if the identity of the author cannot be traced by making reasonable enquiries.

35. Q. What does 'reasonable enquiry' mean?
    A. This is not defined but it would presumably require checking in major catalogues and relevant literary dictionaries, etc.

35a. Q. Supposing the author's identity is established later on?
    A. Once the author's identity is established, then the work is no longer anonymous and the usual rules apply (see question 49a)

36. Supposing the author has used a pseudonym?
    A. Unless you can find out whose pseudonym it is, then the work is counted as anonymous. Like anonymous works, this would require reasonable enquiry, i.e. checking of literary reference works and major library catalogues.

37. Q. Supposing the real identity of the author is established later?
    A. If this happens within the term of copyright then the usual rules apply.

38. Q. What happens if a work definitely has more than one author, but not all their names are known?
    A. Once the name of even one author is known, the work is no longer anonymous.
    Example.   A title page gives: '*Love Poems* by the author of *Love Songs* et al.'. Once the authorship of *Love Songs* has been established, the work is not anonymous, even though the identity of 'et al.' may never be known.

11

39. Q. Supposing the author is given as an organization?
    A. If no person is named as the author the work is treated as anonymous.

40. Q. Who owns the copyright in a periodical issue?
    A. Each author of an article in a periodical issue owns the copyright in that article but the publisher owns the copyright in the issue as a whole.
    Example. Someone writes an article for a periodical. Unless they sign an agreement to the contrary, they retain the copyright in the article and have the right to have it published elsewhere. But they do not have the right simply to photocopy the article as first published and have it republished in that form, nor do they have the right to make copies of the whole periodical issue.

41. Q. If a work was generated by a computer, who counts as the author then?
    A. The person who made the necessary arrangements for creating the work.

42. Q. What about compilations such as directories, timetables, bibliographies and encyclopaedias?
    A. If the work has a personal author then that is the author. So a bibliography compiled by someone is protected just as if it were a book. However, something like the *British National Bibliography* has no personal author so is protected only as an anonymous work.

43. Q. Supposing an encyclopaedia has articles signed by separate people?
    A. Then each article is protected as a separate work.

44. Q. What about material available on CD-ROM?
    A. The same rules apply. If there is no named personal author, the material is protected as an anonymous work.

45. Q. What about databases?
    A. Databases rarely have personal authors! They are therefore regarded as anonymous unless they are fulltext databases where items are separately identified as having authors, such as electronic journals. In this case each item with an author is separately protected.

Duration of copyright

46. Q. Does copyright last for ever?
    A. No. The law limits the time copyright lasts.

47. Q. How long does it last, then?
    A. It depends on the type of material, when it was created and who owns the copyright.

Duration of copyright in published literary, dramatic and musical works

48. Q. What constitutes 'published'?
    A. Published means issuing copies to the public. This in turn means putting into circulation copies not previously put into circulation. Note that the emphasis is on *copies*. Making a single copy does not of itself constitute publication.

49. Q. How long does copyright last for literary, dramatic and musical works?
    A. The copyright in published literary, dramatic and musical works lasts for 50 years from the end of the calendar year in which the author dies. Copyright always expires on 31 December, never in the middle of a year.
    Example. Author died on 5 January 1902. Copyright expires on 31 December 1952. Author died on 29 December 1902. Copyright still expires on 31 December 1952.

49a. Q. Supposing the work is anonymous or has no personal author?
    A. Anonymous works, which includes works which have no personal author such as annual reports of organizations or anything with no identifiable personal author, remain in copyright for 50 years from the end ofthe year in which they are published.

Compilations and periodicals

50. Q. What about works made up of contributions by several people?
    A. The copyright expires separately for each contribution. So the copyright in papers in a conference proceedings expire at different times, depending on when each contributor dies. However, the copyright in the typography will expire sooner (see questions 274-282 on typographical arrangement).

51. Q. When does the copyright in a periodical issue run out?
    A. The copyright in each article will run out 50 years after the death of the author (as for any other published literary work) but the copyright in the periodical issue as a whole (i.e. the typography) will expire 25 years after publication.

Computer-generated works

52. Q. How long does the copyright in a computer-generated work last?
    A. The copyright in a computer-generated work expires 50 years from the end of the year in which the work was made.

Duration of copyright in unpublished literary, dramatic and musical works

53. Q. What if the work is *unpublished*?
    A. If the author died before 1 August 1989 and the work is *not* kept in a library, museum, archive or other institution where it is open to the public for inspection, then copyright expires on 31 December 2039. If the author died on or after 1 August 1989, the work is protected for 50 years from the end of the year in which the author dies.
    Example. Author died 22 November 1975. Copyright expires 31 December 2039. Author dies 3 December 1990. Copyright expires 31 December 2040.

54. Q. What if the author is still alive?
    A. Copyright will last until 50 years after the end of the year in which the author dies, just like a published work.

55. Q. But what about unpublished works that *are* kept in libraries, archives and the rest?
    A. If the work was held by the library or archive before 1 August 1989 and the author has died, then these documents continue to be protected for *either* 50 years after the death of the author *or* 100 years after the time they were made, whichever gives the longer period of protection.
    Example. Author wrote a poem in 1955 and died in 1980. The poem is protected until 31 December 2055 (unless it is published in the meantime, in which case copyright expires at the end of 2030).

14

56. Q. What about anonymous works?
    A. Unpublished anonymous works created before 1 August 1989 are protected until 31 December 2039. Unpublished anonymous works created on or after 1 August 1989 are protected for 50 years after the date on which they are made available to the public.

57. Q. What happens once they are made available to the public?
    A. They are protected for 50 years from the end of the year in which they are made available to the public. This includes, not only publishing, but public performance or broadcasting.

58. Q. Does this mean that unpublished anonymous works can be protected for ever?
    A. Yes, unless they were in existence before 1 August 1989, in which case they are protected only until 31 December 2039. But once made available to the public, the rules above apply.

59. Q. So can unpublished anonymous works ever be published?
    A. Yes, the law allows them to be copied or published if it is reasonable when arrangements are made for publication to suppose that the author has been dead for 50 years.

60. Q. What constitutes 'reasonable'?
    A. This is not defined. Common sense and professional judgement are needed to make a guesstimate as to when a work might have been written.

61. Q. How is the length of copyright worked out if there are several authors?
    A. Copyright lasts until 50 years after the end of the year in which the last one dies. If at least one of the authors is known, then the unknown ones are disregarded.

Crown copyright in literary, dramatic and musical works

62. Q. How long does Crown copyright last?
    A. Crown copyright lasts for 125 years from the year in which the work was created or 50 years from the year in which it was first commercially published.
    Example. A report is prepared in 1930. Its copyright will run out in 2055. But if it is published commercially, say by HMSO, in 1960, then the copyright runs out in 2010.

15

63. Q. What if the author did not die until 1970?
    A. It makes no difference. Length of Crown copyright is linked to date of creation or date of publication, not the human being responsible for creating the work.

64. Q. Supposing some papers were not released because of the 'Thirty Year Rule' and were secret until then?
    A. This makes no difference. Copyright runs from the year in which the work was created.

65. Q. What is Parliamentary copyright?
    A. Parliamentary copyright exists in any work commissioned by either or both Houses of Parliament.

66. Q. How long does it last?
    A. It last for 50 years from the year in which the work was created.

67. Q. Who owns the copyright in a parliamentary bill or Act of Parliament?
    A. The copyright in a bill belongs to whichever House introduced the bill first. When the bill becomes an Act it becomes Crown copyright.

68. Q. Are the publications of other governments protected in the same way?
    A. No. Publications of other governments are protected as if they were ordinary commercial pubications in the UK. In the case of the USA, the US Government claims no copyright in its own publications within the USA and it would seem unlikely that they should be protected in the UK in a way that they are not in the USA. So it is generally assumed that USGPO (United States Government Printing Office) publications are not protected by copyright.

Copying literary, dramatic and musical works
Owner's rights
Copying

69. Q. Does the owner alone have the right to make copies?
    A. Yes, subject to the limitations mentioned later on.

70. Q. Does copying just mean photocopying?
    A. Certainly not. It means copying in any material form. This includes any method of copying including, of course, resetting the type to make a new edition for publication.
    Photocopying. This is clearly copying something and there are special provisions to allow some types of copying for some purposes.
    Electronic copying. It is not allowed to store a work in any electronic form. This includes copying the text onto a computer disk, converting it to electronically readable text by using Optical Character Recognition (OCR) equipment, storing it on CD-ROM or transmitting it by telefacsimile. This also includes making copies of computer programs for any purpose.

71. Q. Is telefacsimile really an infringement?
    A. Technically, yes. The law says that it is an infringement to store a work in electronic form and making copies which are 'transient or incidental to some other use of the work' are an infringement. These are the two things that are done when a fax message is sent. Having said what the law states, it is sometimes the case that common practice is allowed to continue even though technically illegal. Only time will tell what the position of copyright owners on this issue will be.

72. Q. Documents received by fax often fade and disappear. Can the document be further copied as soon as it is received to make a durable copy?
    A. Not legally. This is just a further copy in the fax chain, all of which seem to be infringing copies.

73. Q. What about microforms?
    A. Making a microform is copying and is not permitted without the owner's consent (see questions 388ff).

74. Q. What about copying for the handicapped?
    A. There is no provision for copying for the handicapped in the Act except for subtitling broadcasts or cable programmes for the hard of hearing or persons with other types of handicap. Transcribing works into braille, making sound recordings of books, enlargements for the visually handicapped or the various copies made by print-to-voice machines are all technically infringements. The law permits licensing schemes

for such activities and many copyright owners willingly give their permission, but it should be remembered that this willingness can be eroded if the courtesy of asking first is not observed.

75. Q. Can copies be made for committee meetings?
    A. No. Copying for committees is multiple copying and is not permitted unless the amount copied is less than substantial. However, in many organizations committee copying would be covered by an appropriate licence.

76. Q. Can a slide (or OHP) be made of a page of a book for teaching in a class or giving a lecture?
    A. This would probably be educational copying and is therefore covered by those provisions. If it is for a 'one-off' lecture to, say, a local history group, then it would be in order to make a slide of a page provided that this did not constitute a substantial part of the work.

77. Q. Some books and journals carry a warning that no part of the work can be reproduced, stored, etc. Does this take away the allowances given under the Copyright Act?
    A. This statement has never been tested in law. It is generally thought unlikely that it would stand up in court as it tries to prohibit what the law allows. There is an argument that it constitutes a contract between the publisher and the user about which the user knew perfectly well before buying the book but general opinion is that it is there to frighten rather than be enforced! Actual enforcement of it would be a very difficult thing to do and costly in legal fees to establish as binding. Of course, if it were binding, libraries could refuse to buy the books which would make a considerable difference to publishers' sales.

Issuing copies to the public

78. Q. If issuing copies to the public is an infringement, how can libraries offer a lending service?
    A. The law makes it clear that the right to issue copies to the public only applies to works not previously put into circulation in the UK. So, once copies of a work have been offered for sale through the usual channels, there is no restriction on making them available for loan.

79. Q. Does this freedom apply to all works?
A. No. It is limited to dramatic, musical or artistic works and literary works other than computer programs.

80. Q. Does this idea of issuing copies to the public have any bearing on acquisition of materials?
A. Yes, it does. It is an offence to import anything covered by the Copyright Act into the UK if it would have been an infringement to make a copy of it in the UK or making the copy would be a breach of an exclusive licence granted by the copyright owner. Therefore, it would be an infringement to order a book direct from, say, the USA when the publisher had an exclusive agreement for its distribution with another publisher in the UK. This can cause problems when suppliers holding exclusive UK licences are slow or inefficient and libraries know they can get a better service by going to someone else. Unfortunately this is not allowed. The law says that it is an infringement if the importer (i.e. the library) has 'reason to know' it is an infringing copy. It would be difficult to say that a library had no knowledge of the likelihood of such an exclusive importation arrangement.

Performing the work

81. Q. Libraries and archives are not often involved in public performances. Is this really important for them?
A. Libraries are increasingly involved in cultural activities and some have library theatres so it is important to be aware of the owner's rights, especially when library materials may be utilized to put on performances.

82. Q. Can only the copyright owner authorize performance?
A. Yes.

83. Q. Does performance mean just plays or presentations?
A. No. Performance includes delivery of speeches, lectures or sermons and also includes presentation by visual or audible means.
Example. If the library possesses some poems by a local author, they may not be copied. But it is also an infringement to recite them in public or make a video of someone reciting them in public. Family videos of weddings, for example, may

19

infringe the copyright in the vicar's sermon if he is reading from a prepared text. However, if he is speaking extempore, there is no copyright in his sermon until it has been recorded (on the video). The vicar then owns the copyright in the sermon and the person who shot the video owns the copyright in the video as such!

84. Q. Does this mean that poems cannot be used for public recitation?
    A. Not quite. One person may read a reasonable extract from a copyright work in public provided that the reading is accompanied by sufficient acknowledgement. This would apply to such activities as story time in a children's library.

85. Q. What do the terms 'reasonable extract' and 'sufficient acknowledgement' mean?
    A. They are not defined. Reasonable extract is a matter of judgement. Sufficient acknowledgement would certainly mean saying who wrote the work, when and where it was published, if published at all.

86. Q. Sometimes teachers want to perform plays or hold concerts using copyright library materials. Is this allowed?
    A. Yes provided that only pupils, teachers and other persons directly connected with the educational establishment are present. This does not include mums and dads!

Broadcastng a work

87. Q. Does this have any implications for libraries and archives?
    A. As far as literary, dramatic or musical works go, the main fact to bear in mind is that broadcasting a work is an infringement of the owner's rights. So if a local radio station wished to use some of the library's holdings, such as poems or extracts from local history material for broadcasting purposes, this would not be allowed without permission. This would not apply if the use were solely for news reporting.

Adaptation

88. Q. Does adaptation apply just to plays, novels or similar materials?
    A. No. Several acts count as adaptation. The ones listed by the

20

Act are translation and dramatic-non-dramatic works.

Translation. Translating a work is considered an adaptation and translations shuld not be made without due consideration for the purpose for which they are made and the use to which they will be put.

89. Q. What can be done for a researcher in a laboratory who needs a technical article translated?

A. Provided the translation was entirely for the use of the researcher, fair dealing (see questions 97ff) could be claimed, but if numerous copies of the translation were made then this would be an infringement. Certainly copies of the translation could not be sold.

90. Q. What about a student who wants to translate a play in a foreign language?

A. If the student makes his own translation there is no problem as copying by non-reprographic means for instruction is permitted (see Questions 129ff).

Dramatic-non-dramatic works. It is an infringement to re-write a non-dramatic work as a dramatic one and vice-versa. It is also an infringement to reproduce a story in another form such as pictures.

Example. Someone decides to re-work Alan Ayckbourn's *The Norman Conquests* as a novel. This is an infringement. Equally it would be an infringement to produce a dramatic version of one of Catherine Cookson's novels.

91. Q. Does this restriction include turning a story into pictures, for example for a children's library?

A. Yes. The law specifies that it is not allowed to turn the story into a version wholly or mainly told in the form of pictures suitable for reproduction in a book newspaper or magazine. Although this is obviously aimed at the cartoon market, it has implications for children's libraries and school libraries as well.

92. Q. How does this affect arrangements of musical works?

A. Any arrangement or transcription of a musical work counts as an adaptation.

93. Q. What about texts issued in several languages simultaneously?
    A. Each text attracts its own copyright but they would only be infringing texts if the translations are made without the original owner's consent.

94. Q. Does 'translation' extend to computer 'languages'?
    A. Yes. The law specifically states that changing a program from one computer language to another is an infringement unless this is done incidentally during the running of the program.

95. Q. Supposing an adaptation has been made quite legally. Does that also attract copyright?
    A. Yes and the person who made the adaptation has rights in the adaptation just as the author has in the original work.

Exceptions (allowances)

96. Q. For what purposes can a copyright work be copied without the owner's consent?
    A. There are three reasons listed. The most commonly claimed and most frequently quoted is fair dealing.

Fair dealing

97. Q. What is fair dealing?
    A. Fair dealing is a concept which has never been defined. What it seems to be saying is that there may be good reasons for copying something so long as the copying does not harm the copyright owner but nevertheless benefits either the individual or society generally.

98. Q. Does fair dealing apply to all copyright works?
    A. No. It applies to literary, dramatic, musical or artistic works but not to audiovisual materials such as broadcasts, film, video or sound recordings.

99. Q. How much of a work can be copied under fair dealing?
    A. Nobody knows for certain − it is a matter of individual judgement in each case. What is clear is that until a *substantial* part of a work is copied, there can be no infringement so such defences as fair dealing are not needed.

100. Q. So is there no guidance at all?
   A. In the law, no. Various guidelines have been issued in the past but they are guidelines only. The British Copyright Council has issued a set of guidelines, outlining what they think is fair from an owner's viewpoint.

101. Q. Can a map be copied under fair dealing?
   A. Yes. A map is an artistic work and can be copied under fair dealing.

101a. Q. What about standards such as those produced by the British Standards Institution?
   A. These are also available for fair dealing. The BSI have issued guidelines to help those who need to copy standards. Roughly the proportions they regard as fair are 10% or two pages of small standards.

102. Q. How can anyone judge if copying something is 'fair'?
   A. Look at the *amount* to be copied in conjunction with the *reason* for making the copy. No concrete examples can be given but look at the following situations:

   A student wishes to photocopy a five-verse poem from a collection to study at home; a researcher wishes to publish four out of its five verses in a commercially published criticism of the poet. One is research and private study, the other criticism, both of which are justifications for claiming fair dealing. But the first would seem more likely to be 'fair' than the second. Copying a whole work which has long been out of print and unavailable might be 'fair' but copying the same work just to save buying a copy is obviously not.

103. Q. What are the justifications for fair dealing?
   A. The law recognizes several. The one most commonly cited in libraries is copying for research or private study.

Research or private study

104. Q. Is private study limited to students?
   A. Not at all, if, by 'student' is meant someone in an academic institution. Anyone undertaking training or education or any kind, including leisure courses such as evening classes in

hobbies or holiday languages, can reasonably claim fair dealing as a 'student'.

105. Q. Can any kind of research qualify?
A. Yes. The order of words is important — research or private study — not private study or research. Any sort of research can be the reason for claiming fair dealing, including commercial and industrial research.

106. Q. Why *private* study?
A. Private study is thought of as being done alone. Therefore multiple copying for classroom use cannot be private study and is provided for separately under educational copying (see questions 129ff).

107. Q. Does fair dealing allow the making of more than one copy?
A. If the student or researcher does the copying himself it might be possible to make more than one copy.
Example. Suppose a student has to go on a geography field trip. Two copies of a small portion of a map may be needed — one for use in the field (where it may get muddy or torn) and the other for the file relating to the project. If two copies are made they must be for the personal use only of the person who made them.

108. Q. Supposing the student wants a copy for himself and one for a friend?
A. Not allowed! If any copying is done on behalf of someone else then the person making the copy must not make it if they know that this will result in a copy of substantially the same material being supplied to more than one person at substantially the same time and for substantially the same purpose. But always remember that your institution may have a licence which would allow this.
Example. Three students may make for themselves one copy each of, say, a journal article, for use in a lecture or project. But if one makes copies for himself and his friends then this is an infringement.

109. Q. What do all these 'substantially's' mean?
A. They are not defined but it would seem likely that someone copying pages 9-14 for himself and pages 10-16 for a friend

24

or colleague would have copied 'substantially the *same* material' and that this copying, if done on Monday and Wednesday of the same week for use in the same tutorial or related experiements at the laboratory bench would constitute at substantially the same *time* and for substantially the same *purpose*.

110. Q. What about coin-operated machines then?
     A. Although these are not dealt with specifically, the Act differentiates between copies made by students/researchers themselves and those made for them by other people. Although nothing is said in this context about providing equipment which might be used for infringing purposes it is clear from another part of the Act that it is not an offence to possess equipment which can be used for breach of copyright, as opposed to equipment which can be used only for breach of copyright. It would be foolish of any librarian deliberately to turn a blind eye to copying which was beyond the law, and a suitable notice giving details of what is and is not allowed should be displayed (contact The Library Association for a suggested text). Whether a librarian could actually be held responsible is open to doubt. Any notice should refer to the new Copyright Act and its restrictions. These should also be mentioned in any publicity for the library's services and any user-education courses which are offered. Generally librarians are expected to use their best endeavours to ensure that machines in their care are not used for infringements of copyright.

111. Q. What if the person asks the librarian to do the copying for them?
     A. What the law says, in a rather roundabout way, is that copying by libraries is only fair dealing if the special conditions about copying by libraries are observed. If the library steps outside these conditions then the copying is not fair dealing and becomes an infringement. Copying by libraries is dealt with in detail in questions 132ff.

112. Q. What about downloading from databases?
     A. It will depend on the type of database as already described in question 17a. Downloading from inhouse databases should present no problems because they are often closed systems

25

for use by employees only. Downloading from a desktop PC will usually be under the control of the person in that office but is technically allowed as the work is a literary work. For the the usual type of online database, downloading could not be justified as fair dealing because that database is treated as a cable programme in which there is no fair dealing at all. But for many databases, downloading can usually only be done with a licence from the database owner anyway as part of the contract. Otherwise, it is only allowed in small amounts (i.e. not substantial parts – see question 11). If the database is one like OCLC, which is regarded as a literary work, then downloading for research or private study would be permissible. An intresting sideline of these complexities is that if a database is a cable programme it may be possible to copy the whole of it for private use, i.e. to consult at a more convenient time. Cable programmes are not subject to fair dealing but may be copied in their entirety for time-shifting purposes!

113. Q. What about databases stored on CD-ROM?
     A. CD-ROMs are not cable programmes so any data stored on a CD-ROM is protected as a literary work and is available under the same rules of fair dealing (but not copying for 'time-shifting').

114. Q. Is copying from teletext such as Oracle or Ceefax allowed?
     A. According to the law, no. Such information services are cable television programmes and, as such, are not available or fair dealing purposes. However, the producers often permit copying by means of printers connected to the television receiver and this is then a licence, actual or implied, from the copyright owner. The conditions of any such licence must be complied with and material copied must not be used for commercial republication or other unfair purposes.

Criticism or review

115. Q. What other justifications for fair dealing are there?
     A. An important one for librarians of all kinds is *criticism* or *review*. It is allowed to quote parts of a work when writing critical essays or reviews such as those in the *Library Association record*.

116. Q. How much can be quoted?
     A. Again, it is not stated but the publishers used to say that they felt a single extract of up to 400 words or a series of extracts (none of which was over 300 words) totalling not more than 800 words was not unfair. For poems this was given as 40 lines or not more than 25% of the whole poem. These figures are quoted simply to indicate some thinking on the quantitites that might be involved. The source of the quotations must be given, e.g. the full bibliographic reference in a review is essential as the reviewer may be encouraging the reader to buy a copy! The same is true if a criticism is being written of the writings of a single author. Libraries which prepare their own reviews for the general public or in the form of information bulletins for researchers should note the conditions under which, and to what extent they can quote the works mentioned.

Reporting current events

117. Q. Does this review idea extend to news bulletins?
     A. No. Reporting current events is a separate justification for claiming fair dealing. The production of news bulletins, current events information and similar news items can utilize any news material provided that sufficient acknowledgement of the source is made. Such activities as news clippings services, circulated to staff, are justified on these grounds but each clipping must have the source noted on it. Fair dealing in this context does not extend to photographs.

118. Q. Supposing the news items that are needed include a photograph?
     A. Clearly the law is intended to protect the very considerable investment in photography made by newspapers and without this exception any evening paper could use the photographs of any morning one for its news story. In theory this applies to internal and local news bulletins made from clippings but it is very difficult to exclude a photograph in the middle of a piece of news text. Technically it should be blacked out but this is often done in the photocopying process anyway! The alternative is to retype the necessary text.

119. Q. Supposing the news bulletin is prepared and displayed electronically?
     A. The same rules apply as for a clippings service.

120. Q. Does educational copying apply only to schools and universities?
     A. It depends on which part of the special exceptions are being referred to. Copying by a teacher or pupil for the purposes of instruction other than by a reprographic process is a general allowance as in answering examination questions but other allowances are restricted to 'educational establishments' as defined in the Act.

Educational copying

121. Q. Are the amounts allowed to be copied for educational copying just as vague as in fair dealing?
     A. No, the rules are quite different.

122. Q. What is the difference between copying for educational purposes and copying for private study?
     A. Private study does not mean for classroom use. Educational copying can be for classroom use. All librarians in any organization where teaching takes place should be aware of what is allowed, as the materials in their care are frequently utilized for educational purposes. This is also true for public libraries which are used for project work.

123. Q. Can a teacher or pupil copy anything for use in the classsroom?
     A. A teacher or pupil may copy out all or part of a copyright work in the course of instruction (e.g. a poem) onto the blackboard or into an exercise book for the purposes of instruction but they may not copy it using a reprographic process, i.e. not by photocopying it.

124. Q. Does instruction apply only to schools and universities?
     A. No. Instruction can take place in industrial or commercial training courses, military camps or anywhere else.

124a. Q. What about copying for examinations?
     A. Anything can be copied for the purposes of setting the questions or providing the answers except musical works which may not be photocopied allow the pupil to perform the work.

125. Q. Does anything really mean anything?
     A. Yes, except for musical scores as mentioned above.

126. Q. What if a student needs to include some copyright material in a thesis for a degree?
     A. This would seem to be covered in providing the answers to an examination. There could be problems if the thesis is subsequently copied for other purposes or published.

127. Q. What happens if several children come into the public library, all asking for copies of the same thing for their project?
     A. Only one copy can be provided. However, schools operated by local authorities usually have a licence to copy necesary materials and the teacher should investigate if this will allow the required materials to be copied. A further problem is at what point, if any, someone teaching a continuously assessed courses can claim the right to copy materials for examination purposes.

128. Q. What about including some copyright material in collections put together by teachers?
     A. There are special rules governing this which should be known by the teacher or publisher and not worry the librarian too much. Section 33 of the Act sets out the limits for this sort of publishing.

Copying for educational establishments

129. Q. What counts as an educational establishment?
     A. An educational establishment is defined as
        ● any school
        ● any university allowed to award degrees under Act of Parliament or Royal Charter
        ● any institution empowered to offer further or higher education under the Education (Scotland) Act, 1980, the Education and Libraries (Northern Ireland) Order 1986 or the Education Reform Act (1988). (See SI 98/1068 for exact details).
        ● any theological college

130. Q. Multiple copying is not allowed and fair dealing does not extend to classroom copying, so what can be done for teachers

who need multiple copies of parts of works for use in instruction. Surely they do not have to rely on writing everything out by hand?

A.   No! The Act allows one of two ways forward. If a licence is obtainable to cover the needed materials, then that licence should be taken out and adhered to. All local authorities and many universities have taken out such a licence and the first thing is to check what it covers and what it allows. If no licence is obtainable then the law allows that up to 1% of a work may be copied for classroom use in any three-month period specified by the Act. (The Act actually lays down that these periods are fixed as 1 January to 31 March, 1 April to 30 June, 1 July to 30 September and 1 October to 31 December.) These allowances may not be claimed if the person doing the copying knew, or ought to have known, that a licensing scheme was available but no licensing scheme is allowed to restrict copying to below these very small limits.

131. Q.   Can the library do this copying on behalf of the teacher/lecturer?
      A.   Yes. But make sure the terms of the licence are known before agreeing to do such copying.

Libraries and archives

Copying published literary, dramatic or musical works

This is the most important limitation on owner's rights as far as librarians and archivists are concerned. The main user group mentioned in the Act is libraries and archives. The special exceptions for libraries and archives apply to literary, dramatic and musical works but not to artistic works.

132. Q.   Are the terms 'library' and 'archive' defined?
      A.   No. There are definitions of *prescribed* libraries and archives but not libraries and archives generally.

133. Q.   Are the terms interchangeable?
      A.   No. Specific allowances are given to libraries and archives separately.

134. Q.   So what are libraries allowed to do that is special?
      A.   Quite a lot. Firstly, they can supply copies of works to their users.

Copying for users

135. Q. Is there a limit on how much of a work can be copied for a user?

 A. Yes. There are different limits for different kinds of material. In the case of a periodical, no user can be supplied with a copy of more than one article in the same periodical issue.

136. Q. Can the user have more than one copy of the same article?

 A. Not under any circumstances.

137. Q. Supposing the volume of separate issues has been bound, how does this affect copying?

 A. The law is not specific but it seems likely that the interpretation would be that not more than one article could be copied from any one original periodical part as issued to the public. The subsequent binding by the library would, in any case, reduce the freedom to copy for the user, if this view were taken as the bound volume would become the 'issue'. As this would change the amount allowed to be copied by an action beyond the copyright owner's control, it is unlikely that this view would be taken. The original form of publication is therefore what really counts.

138. Q. Supposing the article includes some drawings or photographs. It is allowed to copy these as well?

 A. Yes. If an article is copied for someone, then it is allowed to copy any accompanying illustrations. Accompanying is an important word. If the article is in, say, an art journal and is supplemented by high-quality plates of paintings just to further illustrate the artist's work, these may not be copied unless they are intrinsic to the understanding of the text.

139. Q. What counts as an 'article'?

 A. Unfortunately this term is defined but in very general terms. An article, in the context of an article in a periodical, means an item of any description.

140. Q. Does this include things like advertisements, the title page, contents page or index?

 A. Yes, so the user should not really be supplied with an article from an issue and also the contents page.

31

141. Q. What about making copies of contents pages and circulating them for information amongst staff?
     A. This is not allowed. In the first place, it is multiple copying and secondly the library cannot make copies for people unless they sign the declaration form first.

142. Q. So is this not allowed at all?
     A. It would be possible to circulate *one* copy of the contents page amongst staff, provided one of them asked for the copy in the first place. Alternatively, it is a good idea to write to the publishers concerned and ask if they will permit this. Most say they will as it is good advertising for their journals but some take the view that it could encourage related copying (i.e. more than one copy requested by different people at the same time for the same purpose).

143. Q. Supposing the user wants two articles from the same issue?
     A. Only one can be provided. However, it might be possible for the user to claim fair dealing if the user borrowed the periodical issue and made the copies himself. This would then require a fair dealing defence so the copying should not be of such an extent that this was not a plausible defence.

144. Q. What constitutes a periodical?
     A. This is not defined. The really difficult area is the monograph published as part of a series. When a series becomes a periodical is not easy to determine. However, the term periodical should not be used when the work under consideration is plainly a monograph in a numbered series, probably so published for the publisher's convenience.

145. Q. If a publisher charges a higher rate for a library subscription to a periodical, can more copying be done?
     A. No, unless the publisher has specifically stated this in the publicity, catalogues or in a specific letter to the library.

Abstracts

146. Q. Does the abstract that goes with a journal article have a separate copyright?
     A. Yes. It is a distinct work which can stand alone — otherwise it is not really an abstract.

32

147. Q. Can it be copied with the article?
   A. Yes. The law states that such abstracts can be copied freely unless there is a licensing scheme which covers them, in which case you must belong to the scheme to copy the abstracts.

148. Q. Can they be used in information bulletins?
   A. Yes. They can be duplicated, printed, given away or sold, either freely or by licence.

149. Q. Does a newspaper count as a periodical?
   A. It would seem logical to assume so although the law says nothing specifically about newspapers.

150. Q. Can articles be copied from newspapers?
   A. Yes. There is no problem.

151. Q. But to copy one article from a newspaper often involves incidentally copying another, or at least part of another. What is the position then?
   A. Technically only the article actually required can be copied. To be perfectly correct all other parts of the page should be blanketed! But this would be incidental copying, really as an accident or done simply in the normal process of doing what is allowed. *If* a case were brought, it might be possible to argue, by analogy, incidental copying similar to that allowed for artistic works in photographs (see question 298) but that is only an opinion.

152. Q. Does the copying of articles extend to conference proceedings?
   A. It will depend on the nature of the conference publication. Many annual or more frequent conferences appear simply as 'Proceedings of the *x*th conference on . . .' and could be viewed as a serial. Others with no clear numbering, or with monographic titles, must be treated as books.

153. Q. What about technical reports in a numbered series?
   A. Generally these must be treated as separate monographs.

154. Q. Supposing the periodical issue consists of just one article?
   A. The law specifically states that *one* article may be copied

from a periodical issue. It seems clear that this allows the copying of an article if it constitutes the entire issue of a periodical although any other material in that issue, such as title page, advertisements or other ephemeral material must not be copied.

155. Q. What about SDI services?
    A. The arrangement whereby the librarian scans various information services for material that is considered relevant to the resarches of library users and then obtains copies of these items and passes them on to users without being asked for them is an infringement.

156. Q. What can be done for researchers in this situation?
    A. There is no reason why a librarian may not produce a current awareness bulletin from which staff select and request items they require but they must ask for items, not have them sent gratuitously.

157. Q. What about libraries in industry and commerce?
    A. There is no way that this system can be operated within the law. The librarian is not entitled to request material from another library but only on behalf of the reader. Therefore the librarian can only identify material of potential interest and draw it to the attention of the researcher. The researcher must then request the item from the librarian who simply forwards the request to a prescribed library if it is not held in the requestor's own library.

158. Q. What about books (monographs)?
    A. The librarian may supply one copy of not more than a reasonable proportion of a book to a reader.

159. Q. What constitutes a 'reasonable' proportion?
    A. This is not defined. However, it is safe to assume that a reasonable proportion is larger than a substantial part because if less than a substantial part had been copied, there would be no need to claim any defence. Like substantial part and fair dealing this is a matter of individual judgement.

160. Q. Supposing a book consists mostly of photographs and plates?
    A. Each item will be a copyright item in its own right and must

be treated as such. This does not apply to illustrations accompanying material which can be copied under fair dealing but the illustration must accompany the text. Text which accompanies illustrations will not count for this allowance.

Restrictions on copying for readers

161. Q. Are there other restrictions?
   A. Yes. The librarian can copy an article from a periodical or part of a published work only if the user signs a declaration form which states that

   (a) a copy has not previously been supplied
   (b) the copy will not be used except for research or private study and that a copy will not be supplied to any other person
   (c) that to the best of [his] knowledge no person with whom [he] works or studies has made or intends to make at about the same time a request for substantially the same material for substantially the same purpose.

   In addition, the user is required to pay a sum which will cover not only the cost of making the copy but make a general contribution towards the running of the library.

162. Q. Those 'substantially's have turned up again. Are they defined in this part of the Act any better than in the other?
   A. In a word, no. The same uncertainty applies (see question 109).

163. Q. Can a user really be expected to sign a statement about the intentions of other people?
   A. No, that is not what is being asked. The user signs to say that *to the best of his knowledge* nobody else is going to ask for copies of substantially the same material. . . . Thus he can be in complete ignorance and truthfully sign the form.

164. Q. Does this declaration have to be made when the request is made?
   A. No. But it must be made before the copy is handed over. These two actions often coincide in smaller libraries but in large libraries or public libraries there is often a waiting time between the request and the arrival of the copy. It is perfectly

in order to obtain the signed declaration at the time the request is made but it must be borne in mind that in some circumstances a copy may not be supplied but the original lent instead. In this case the declaration is superfluous. On the other hand the requestor may not be aware that the request will be fulfilled by a photocopy so it would be reasonable not to ask for a signature until the document was handed over. However, when copies are obtained from *other libraries*, this procedure cannot be followed unless the requesting library is a prescribed library (see questions 199ff on interlibrary copying).

165. Q. What happens when requests are received by telephone or letter?
     A. The request can be processed but the copies cannot be handed over until the declaration form has been signed. This may well cause rather long correspondence but there is no easy way round this.

166. Q. Can the declaration be sent by fax?
     A. Yes. Fax is widely regarded in legal circles as an adequate substitute for the actual signed document. Much larger transactions than library photocopies are settled in this way!

167. Q. Must payment be made before the copies are handed over?
     A. No but payment must be made at some point. (See questions 188-189).

168. Q. What if the person making the request lives overseas?
     A. This makes no difference. Even though the amounts may be small, payment cannot be avoided.

169. Q. What if something is required urgently?
     A. The obvious solution is for the requestor to come to the library in person. With the increasing use of fax machines, the declaration can be faxed. Failing that, they could find a helpful prescribed library nearby them who would make the request on their behalf as prescribed libraries do not need to make declarations except for items mentioned in questions 199ff. The user would make his declaration to the librarian of the prescribed library who was actually making the request.

170. Q. Is there a standard form in which this declaration must be made?
A. Yes. The text is published in Statutory Instrument 89/1212 Schedule 2 Form A and also at the end of this book.

171. Q. So, as long as these conditions are met, can any librarian copy for a user?
A. No, it is not so simple. The user must sign a declaration but, in addition, the librarian must be satisfied that the requirements of two or more people are not:

(*a*) similar
(*b*) related

and that no person is furnished with

(*a*) more than one copy
(*b*) more than one article from a periodical issue or more than a reasonable part of any other published work.

172. Q. Can the librarian rely on the user's honesty when signing the declaration form?
A. Basically, yes.

173. Q. Supposing the user signs the declaration and it turns out to be untrue?
A. Librarians cannot be expected to know the inner motives of their users and the law recognizes this. The librarian may rely on a signed declaration from the reader as to all the points listed unless the librarian is aware that it is false in any particular way.

174. Q. Then who is liable if the user signs a false declaration?
A. The law specifies that it is the user who would be guilty as if he had made the copy himself.

175. Q. How can a librarian know that a copy has not been obtained from another library?
A. That is not possible. But the declaration which the user signs specifically states that the user has not been supplied with a copy by 'you or any other librarian'.

176. Q. Can the user give his copy to someone else?
   A. Perhaps. But the declaration says that the reader will not *use* the copy except for research or private study. Giving it away could be regarded as using it for other purposes but this is open to question. What is clear is that if he gave it to someone else and they used it for any other purpose, this would make it an infringing copy. But the reader signs a declaration to say he will not give a copy of it to anyone else, i.e. he will not give a copy of the copy with which he has been supplied to anyone else. In other words, he will not photocopy the photocopy.

177. Q. If he gives the copy to someone else, can he have another from the library?
   A. No, because he must sign to say he has not previously been supplied with a copy.

178. Q. Supposing he genuinely lost the previous copy?
   A. The librarian cannot legally supply another. Readers should not be so careless! However, there seems to be nothing to stop him borrowing the item and making a further copy for his private use. In this case, the copying would fall outside the provisions for libraries and become fair dealing.

179. Q. What is the position if a second user also genuinely asks for the same material as the first, equally ignorant of the request by the first person?
   A. If the librarian is aware of this the second person cannot be supplied with a copy.

180. Q. That seems rather unfair on the second user.
   A. Perhaps so. But the idea is that he should share the first person's copy.

181. Q. Do all these references to the 'librarian' really mean only the person in charge of the library?
   A. No. The law says that references to the librarian include a person acting on behalf of the librarian.

182. Q. Can any librarian copy for someone under these conditions?
   A. Yes. There is no discrimination in favour of prescribed libraries in this area.

183. Q. Can any librarian make a copy for any member of the public?
A. It would appear so although it might be difficult for a member of the general public to satisfy all the conditions if that person asked for a copy from the librarian of an industrial or commercial company.

184. Q. What about information brokers who obtain documents from libraries for their clients?
A. If a broker goes to a library in person to ask for a copy to be made and that copy is for a client, the librarian should not make the copy unless the broker can produce a signed copy of the appropriate declaration form. The broker cannot sign a declaration that the document is required by the broker himself for the purposes of research or private study.

185. Q. Could the broker be regarded as acting on behalf of the librarian?
A. Not really because the broker will actually be asking the library for the copies.

186. Q. Could the broker collect the properly signed forms on behalf of a client and bring them to the library to request copies?
A. This would seem a possible solution but the librarian would need to be sure that the signatures on the forms were actually those of the persons requiring the copies.

187. Q. Can the broker charge for the copies?
A. No. The broker can recoup the cost through charging for other services but not for the copy itself.

188. Q. Must all library users pay?
A. Yes. All copying done on behalf of someone else by librarians must be paid for.

189. Q. Supposing circumstances are such that the user cannot pay?
A. Legally, some way must be found for payment to be made. For example, employees in a company or researchers in a university should pay when copies are made for them. They could be reimbursed by the institution later or a voucher system could be introduced but some kind of payment should be made.

190. Q. Is the amount specified?
     A. Not directly, but it must be a sufficient amount to cover not only the cost of making the copy but also contributing towards the general running costs of the library.

191. Q. Is photocopying subject to VAT?
     A. Yes, although the amounts on individual copies may be so small that a per-page charge which is calculated to include the VAT is probably the most practicable way to collect this.

192. Q. Do users of public libraries have to pay?
     A. Yes. It might be argued that the payment of local community charge is a contribution to the general expense of the library but that would only apply to residents of the authority running the library and users must still pay for the actual cost of the photocopy.

193. Q. What about students?
     A. They should pay like eveyone else although, again, it could be argued that part of their fee is for the general upkeep of the library. Again, they still have to pay for the copies.

194. Q. What about people in industrial and commercial companies? Can they really be expected to pay?
     A. Yes. Payment each time a copy is made need not be made at the time, but the library should raise an invoice to the user at regular intervals. Internal accounting procedures may allow this to be paid from a department within a company to the library but there is no way that payment can be avoided.

195. Q. How can a librarian tell if the requirements of two or more users are 'similar'?
     A. Similar is defined only in terms of substantially the same material at substantially the same time and for substantially the same purpose!

196. Q. So is there really no guidance as to what these terms mean?
     A. No. It is fairly easy to give examples of what *would* be regarded as substantial as in question 11 but it is very difficult to say what would *not* be regarded as substantial in these terms.

197. Q. How can a librarian tell if requirements are related?
      A. This is a lot easier. Related is defined a 'those persons receive instruction to which material is relevant at the same time and place.' This is to stop classroom copying by libraries in educational establishments.

198. Q. Can a library download records from a database?
      A. That depends on the nature of the database. If it is a literary work (see question 17a) then small numbers of records could be downloaded if the library is a prescribed library. If the database is not a literary work then such downloading is not allowed. However, access to most databases is controlled through licence, and copyright owners can check the amount of downloading taking place and make charges accordingly.

Interlibrary copying

199. Q. Can libraries supply photocopies through interlibrary loan arrangements?
      A. Yes, in certain circumstances.

200. Q. Can any library take part in these arrangements?
      A. It depends whether the library is being asked for copies or is asking for copies.

201. Q. Which libraries can supply copies, then?
      A. *Any* library in the United Kingdom can make and supply photocopies of material in its collections.

202. Q. What about receiving copies?
      A. Only *prescribed libraries* may request and receive copies.

203. Q. What is a prescribed library?
      A. A prescribed library is carefully defined as:

      ● any library administered by a library authority in England and Wales;
      ● a statutory library authority in Scotland or an Education and Library Board in Northern Ireland;
      ● The British Library, the National Libraries of Scotland and Wales, the Bodleian Library (Oxford), and the University Library, Cambridge;
      ● libraries in educational establishments;

41

- parliamentary and government libraries;
- local authority libraries;
- any library whose purpose is to facilitate or encourage study of a wide range of given topics. (See question 207);
- any library whose purpose is to facilitate or encourage study of a wide range of given topics (see question 207), and which is outside the United Kingdom.

204. Q. What constitutes an educational establishment?
     A. Educational establishment is defined broadly as any school, college, polytechnic or university in the public sector but for specific details see Statutory Instrument 89/1068

205. Q. Is a government library restricted to those in Civil Service Departments?
     A. No, the definition includes any library conducted for or administered by an agency which is administered by a Minister of the Crown. So, for example, the library of a NHS hospital would count as a government library. The library of a private hospital would not.

206. Q. What is the difference between a public library and the library administered by a local authority?
     A. This latter category is intended for those libraries which act as libraries for departments of local or county councils. For example, many planning or environmental health departments have their own libraries and some councils have a members' library for councillors' benefit.

207. Q. What is this wide range of given topics just mentioned?
     A. It is actually listed as 'bibliography, education, fine arts, history, languages, law, literature, medicine, music, philosophy, religion sciences (including natural and social science) or technology.'

208. Q. What exactly does 'conducted for profit' mean?
     A. This is a very important phrase as it does not simply apply to the library itself but includes the organization which owns or administers the library. So the library of a major industrial company may well not be conducted for profit but the owning company certainly is and the library is not therefore a prescribed library.

209. Q. What about charities?
     A. The library of a charity may or may not be a prescribed
        library, depending on the purpose of the charity. If it is a
        charity whose aims are primarily to facilitate or encourage
        the study of the range of topics stated, then the library can
        claim to be prescribed. If the charity is mainly concerned
        with other purposes such as improving social welfare,
        advancing human rights or promoting particular points of
        view or if the charity operates commercially, then it cannot
        claim to be prescribed.

210. Q. What about libraries of learned societies?
     A. Many of these will qualify as the primary aim of the society
        will be to facilitate or encourage the study of the relevant
        subject. But, like charities, it will depend on the aims of the
        society administering the library.

211. Q. What about private libraries?
     A. Some private libraries could say they are conducted for profit
        and in that case they cannot qualify, but others are charitable
        in status and again it will depend on the nature of the charity.

212. Q. Can anything be copied by prescribed libraries?
     A. No. There are restrictions on both periodical articles and
        books (monographs).

Periodical articles

213. Q. What are the restrictions for periodical articles?
     A. Firstly, no library may be supplied with more than one copy
        of an article. Secondly, no library may be supplied with a
        copy of more than one article from a periodical issue unless
        the requesting library also supplies a written statement to the
        effect that it is a prescribed library and does not know, and
        has not been able by reasonable enquiry to find out the name
        and address of someone entitled to authorize the making of
        the copy. Thirdly, the requesting library must pay.

214. Q. What does 'reasonable inquiry' mean?
     A. This is not defined but it should be remembered that as the
        library which is being asked to make the copy must hold the
        periodical it is quite possible that the requesting library could

obtain the required information from the supplying library and even more likely that the supplying library could find this out anyway. However, if the periodical is published by a company now out of business or in a remote corner of the world and does not reply to correspondence, then the copies can be made.

215. Q. Many requests will be to satisfy readers' needs. What if two readers in the same library ask for the same material through interlibrary loan?

    A. The requesting library can make only one request and the copy received must be shared by the two readers unless the librarian is satisfied that their requirements are not related and each signs a separate declaration to this effect. This is true on two counts: firstly, the library is not entitled to receive more than one copy; secondly, the library is not allowed to make two copies of a work for two (or more) people who require it at substantially the same time and for substantially the same purpose.

216. Q. Supposing there are two students at a university requiring the copies for totally different courses?

    A. This does not seem to matter. They still require them for substantially the same purpose and they are receiving instruction in the same place although this might not apply if two lecturers asked for the same material for totally different courses.

217. Q. Is a prescribed library allowed to keep the copies and add them to stock?

    A. Yes. This is one way that the problem of two people requiring the same material can be overcome. Reader A borrows the photocopy and returns it. Reader B then borrows it in the same way as any other library materials.

218. Q. What if a copy is lost or destroyed?

    A. A second copy cannot be asked for as prescribed libraries may only request one copy and there is no time limit on this. However, it is a nice point that, if the photocopy had been placed in the permanent collection (see question 236), then might the library be able to request a replacement at some distant date?

219. Q. Can the library subsequently dispose of the copy to another library?
A. Only to another prescribed library which did not already have a copy of the material in question and which paid the stipulated amount including a contribution to the general running costs of the library.

220. Q. Suppose the library sold off its collection. What should happen to the photocopies?
A. They should either be sold to another prescribed library (which should pay the cost of making the copies, plus a contribution to the running expenses of the library) or destroyed.

Monographs

221. Q. What are the restrictions on copying books (monographs)?
A. One prescribed library may copy *all or part* of a work for another prescribed library but only if the requesting library also supplies a written statement to the effect that it is a prescribed library and does not know, and has not been able by reasonable enquiry to find out, the name and address of someone entitled to authorize the making of the copy.

222. Q. What does 'reasonable inquiry' mean?
A. See question 214 for detailed comments on this phrase and its implications. In the case of books it would not be sufficient to simply check *Books in Print* or some similar guide to currently-available materials because the law requires reasonable inquiry into the ownership of the copyright not just availability in print.

Restrictions

223. Q. Must libraries pay for interlibrary copying?
A. Yes, in exactly the same way as individual users must pay libraries for copies made for them, i.e. the cost must include not only making the copy but a general contribution to the running expenses of the library.

224. Q. Can the fees be waived?
A. No. This is not allowed.

225. Q. Does payment using British Library forms fulfil this requirement?

A. Yes. The voucher system operated by the British Library is a monetary system and actual value is transferred when the vouchers are exchanged so payment is made.

226. Q. Does interlibrary copying attract VAT?

A. Yes, just as copying for individuals does.

227. Q. How can a library which is not a prescribed library obtain a photocopy on interlibrary loan?

A. Libraries that are not prescribed libraries may not request material from other libraries. Only prescribed libraries and individuals can request material from other libraries.

228. Q. What can those working in industry and commerce, and other non-prescribed libraries, do for users who want copies of documents not held in their library?

A. Individuals are entitled to receive copies, provided they have signed the appropriate declaration form. They are entitled to receive copies from librarians (and any library in the UK is a prescribed library for the purposes of *supplying* copies) or persons acting on behalf of librarians. Therefore it would seem logical that a library user in a non-prescribed library may request a document from the librarian, who in turn requests it from another librarian, at which point the first librarian is acting on behalf of the second and supplies the copy for the use of the original user (not the librarian). Thus the user can obtain a copy of a document not immediately available in his own library. An alternative is for the librarian of the prescribed library to arrange to act as an agent on behalf of the non-prescribed library to which the request will be sent for the user, but this is rather tortuous and not altogether clearly allowed. In either case the non-prescribed librarian is simply the agent (letter-box) for the prescribed library. All this is rather complex so an example might help.

Example. A researcher in Anybros Ltd asks the librarian of that company for a copy of an article from a periodical which Anybros do not take. The librarian of Anybros cannot apply to Sometown University because the library of Anybros is not a prescribed library. So he applies, acting simply as the letter-box for the researcher, who is entitled to ask for copies from Sometown University under fair dealing library provisions. The librarian of Anybros Ltd must be aware that Sometown University Library see the librarian as acting as their agent to handle requests from individuals which are to be passed to Sometown University. This would require, if not a proper agreement, at least some kind of letter of intent and the arrangement cannot be inferred from the general situation of the Copyright Act itself.

These two models are just ideas which might be allowed. There are a number of reasons why they might not but only a test case would settle the issue one way or the other.

229. Q. Can the non-prescribed library keep the copy?
    A. Under no circumstances. Copies can only be requested for the use of individuals and must be handed over to them permanently.

230. Q. What happens if the user no longer requires the copy and subsequently gives these copies back to the library?
    A. The library must refuse to take them unless it is a prescribed library.

231. Q. Must they be destroyed then?
    A. Not necessarily. The user is entitled to keep the copy and may add it to his files of other papers. These are often then deposited in an appropriate department of the institution or company. A suitable registry would need to be used for depositing such material but it must not be a library or archive as such and its primary purpose must not be to store copies of copyright material! Neither should it be administered in any way by the librarian.

232. Q. What about brokers who request items through interlibrary loan for their clients?
    A. The broker cannot easily do this as he is certainly not a prescribed library. However, he could, as mentioned in question 228, simply be acting as a letter-box for his client as an individual or he could enter into a proper agreement with a prescribed library to be their agent. Again, all this is not at all clear under the Act.

233. Q. Can the broker charge for the copies obtained through interlibrary loan?

A. No. This would be dealing in the copies which is an infringement. The broker can, however, charge for other services and so recoup the costs necessarily incurred in obtaining the document through interlibrary loan.

Copying for preservation

234. Q. Can library and archival materials be copied to preserve the original?

A. Yes, in certain libraries and archives and under certain circumstances.

235. Q. Which libraries and archives are concerned?

A. Firstly, for supplying copies for preservation and replacement, any library or archive in the United Kingdom. Secondly, for requesting and receiving copies, any prescribed library or any archive not conducted for profit and not forming part of, or admininistered by, an organization conducted for profit. Note this is different for archives from the limitations on libraries which set out specific classes of library. So the archive of a charity whose primary aim was, say, social welfare, would be a prescribed archive but the library of the same charity would not.

So, the archive of a major chemical company could copy material to replace that in a university library but the reverse is not true.

236. Q. Can anything in a prescribed library or archive be copied?

A. No. Firstly, material has to be in the permanent collection of the library or archive. Therefore, it is not allowed to borrow a document from somewhere else, put it into the collection on a temporary basis, copy it and then return it to the original owner. This is particularly important for collections which are deposited for limited periods (e.g. lifetime of the owner). Secondly, the material has to be in the permanent collection and available only for reference on the premises or for loan only to other libraries or archives. Thirdly, it must not be reasonably practicable for the librarian or archivist to purchase a copy.

237. Q. Can libraries or archives copy their own materials under these conditions?
A. Yes, so long as the conditions mentioned are fulfilled.

238. Q. Can one library or archive copy for another?
A. Yes, provided that the requesting library or archive provides a declaration to the effect that it is a prescribed library or archive and it has not been practicable to purchase a copy, and that the copy is required as a replacement for an item in the permanent collection which has been lost, damaged or destroyed. In addition, the requesting library or archive must pay as set out in questions 161 and 188.

239. Q. Once the material has been copied, can it be used like other materials in a library or archive?
A. Yes, provided that it is added to the permanent collection.

240. Q. So what about books or periodicals in general lending collections which are falling apart or are lost?
A. These cannot qualify for copying under these special regulations. Replacement copies must be bought from the publisher, where available, or a copy obtained from another library if the conditions for that are met (i.e. publisher cannot be traced and copy not easily purchased).

241. Q. For exactly which reasons can material be copied for preservation?
A. The law allows copying in order to replace an item in the permanent collection so that the original can be saved from constant use either by withdrawing it altogether or relieving the amount of use made of each copy or for replacing material in another library or archive which has been lost, damaged or destroyed. Clearly a library or archive cannot replace material in its own collection in this way since, if it is lost or destroyed, it is not there to copy!

242. Q. Could a prescribed library or archive obtain a copy of a work from a library if the work was in the general lending collection?
A. Only material in a reference collection such as local history or general reference can be copied for preservation purposes in either that or another library. Works on the shelves for loan cannot be copied for replacement in other libraries or archives.

Computer programs

243. Q. Are computer programs treated exactly like other literary works?
     A. Not entirely. Although computer programs are classed as literary works, there are some special conditions which apply.

244. Q. If there is rental right in computer programs, can libraries lend them?
     A. Only if there is a licensing scheme available.

245. Q. Does this apply to computer programs which have been printed out?
         A. Probably not. The Act includes computer programs with sound recordings and films which implies the legislators had them in mind as audiovisual materials. If it were not allowed to 'rent' computer programs in printed form, many popular computer magazines would have to be withdrawn from library shelves.

246. Q. What happens if the library has a computer program or other electronic material which becomes unusable for technical reasons? Can it be copied so that it can continue to be used?
     A. Yes, provided that the conditions of purchase do not prohibit such copying and the original copy must not be retained, otherwise it becomes an infringing copy.

Copying unpublished works

247. Q. Can unpublished materials in a library be copied for users?
     A. Yes, under certain conditions?

248. Q. What are the conditions?
     A. Firstly, the work has not been published before the document was deposited. Secondly, copying may not take place if the author has prohibited this.
         Example. An author writes a novel and deposits the manuscript with the local public library. Subsequently he arranges to have it published. The public library is entitled to copy the manuscript (within the limits mentioned in questions 250ff) even though the text has become a published novel. However, if the author has his book published and then deposits the manuscript with the local public library, no copying of it is allowed.

50

249. Q. Can the librarian or archivist plead ignorace of the fact that the author had prohibited copying?

A. Not really. The law says that copies may not be made when the author has prohibited this and the librarian or archivist knows, *or ought to know*, that this is the case. Therefore, it is sensible to keep a register of deposited unpublished material with notes on any items which the author has prohibited the library or archive from copying.

250. Q. Can whole works be copied, or only parts?

A. The law allows copying of the whole of a document.

251. Q. Can unpublished works be copied for anyone?

A. Yes, provided that the reader signs a declaration to say that the documents are required only for research or private study.

252. Q. Can they have more than one copy?

A. No person may have more than one copy of any work.

253. Q. Do users have to pay?

A. Yes, they must pay just as in question 161 and 188.

254. Q. Do the restrictions on not supplying copies to more than one person for substantially the same purpose at substantially the same time apply?

A. No, these restrictions are not laid down for unpublished works.

255. Q. Is there a standard declaration form as for published materials?

A. Yes. The text is published in Statutory Instrument 89/1212 Schedule 2 Form B and also at the end of this book.

256. Q. Can copies be supplied from one archive to another?

A. No. Copying between prescribed libraries applies only to published works and the sections on unpublished works allow only copying for individuals. It would seem likely, by analogy with a user of a non-prescribed library, that the user of a prescribed library or archive could ask that library or archive to apply on his behalf for a copy of an unpublished work but he would have to sign the appropriate declaration form, pay the required amount and also retain the copy for personal use, not present it to the library or archive which has acted as intermediary for him.

51

Copying as a condition of export

257. Q. Supposing a library or archive contains material which is still in copyright but is of considerable national interest and it is decided to sell this abroad. Can anything be done to copy it before it is taken out of the country?

   A. Sometimes, yes. If the condition of export is that a copy is made to be retained in this country it is not an infringement to make the copy or to receive it to be kept in a library or archive.

Public Administration

258. Q. Are there any other reasons for being allowed to copy?

   A. Yes. The other main reason is what the Act calls public administration.

259. Q. What does 'public administration' cover?

   A. Not as much as it would at first seem! Basically it covers:
   Parliamentary proceedings
   judicial proceedings
   Royal Commission
   statutory inquiry

260. Q. What can be copied?

   A. There are no limits. The Act says 'Copyright is not infringed by anything done for the purposes of Parliamentary or judicial proceedings.' The only qualification is a further allowance to the effect that if anything is copied for the proceedings and subsequently published in those proceedings this is not itself an infringement of copyright.

Material open to public inspection

261. Q. Many libraries contain registers of various kinds and often act as a public information point for local authority activity such as planning applications. Can any of this material be copied?

   A. When material is open to the public as part of a statutory requirement, or is on a statutory register, any material in it which contains factual information can be copied without infringing the copyright in it as a literary work so long as this is done with the authority of the appropriate person and copies are not issued to the public.

262. Q. Does making a copy for a member of the public constitute 'issuing copies to the public'.
    A. No. Making single copies for individuals in this way is outside the definition of 'issuing copies to the public'.

263. Q. What constitutes factual information?
    A. Exactly that. Anything in the material which is opinion or argument for or against a case would not be covered by this allowance.

264. Q. Does this include maps and plans?
    A. No. The clause is specific about literary works only.

265. Q. Supposing someone wants to inspect some documents in this class but lives some way away and cannot come to consult the documents?
    A. Any amount of the material may be copied for such persons provided that the appropriate person gives authorization

266. Q. Does this apply to maps and plans as well?
    A. Yes. There is no restriction on the material which may be copied for those needing it sent to them to exercise their rights. However, to prevent misuse, any maps supplied for this purpose must be marked with a statement to the effect that the maps had been supplied under the Copyright Act for the purposes of consulting publicly available material and must not be further copied without permission. The full text of this statement, which must be used as it stands, is printed in SI 89/1099. [Interestingly, the Statutory Instrument refers to statutory registers but the relevant sections of the Act do not.]

267. Q. Does this also apply to statutory registers such as registers of voters?
    A. Apparantly not, because no mention is made of statutory registers in the relevant section. However, the Statutory Instrument does refer specially to statutory registers in this section, so it is unclear just what is allowed.

268. Q. Do these regulations apply only to United Kingdom materials?
    A. Mostly, yes. The two exceptions are material made open to

the public by the European Patent Office and the World Intellectual Property Organization, both intended to assist the process of patent registration.

269. Q. Who is an 'appropriate person'?
      A. An appropriate person is the person who is required to make the material open to the public or the person maintaining the register. Such persons can authorize libraries and others to make copies as described above.

270. Q. What about material which constitutes public records?
      A. Any material which constitutes public records under the appropriate Public Records Acts which are open to public inspection can be copied and copies supplied to anyone, with the authority of the appropriate officer as appointed under the relevant Acts of Parliament.

271   Q. What if an Act of Parliament actually requires that something be copied for the processes of law?
      A. If the copying is a required part of an Act of Parliament then it is not an infringement of copyright.

Typographical arrangements of published editions

272. Q. Is there copyright in the actual typeface of a work?
      A. There is copyright in the typeface of an artistic work.

273. Q. So can this copyright prevent the work from being copied?
      A. No. The law specifically states it is not an infringement of the copyright in a typeface to use it to print or do other things in the normal course of publishing. It is protected only in areas of importation and equipment used to make typefaces which are infringing. Once used for printing it is not an infringement touse or copy it.

274. Q. What is typographical copyright?
      A. Every published work has two copyrights: one in the actual content of the text and the other in the printed layout of the page.

275. Q. Who counts as the author of the typographical arrangement of a work?
      A. The publisher.

276. Q. How long does typographical coypright last?

A. Typographical copyright lasts for 25 years from the end of the year in which the work is published.

277. Q. So when does the copyright on a published work actually expire?

A. There are two expiry dates. The earlier will always be the typographical coyright one which runs out 25 years after first publication. However, the author's copyright continues until 50 years after death. So the copyright in a book runs out in two stages. This does nothing to help people who want to copy it within that 25 year period, of course. However, it does allow republication by another publisher if the author has retained his own copyright and not assigned it to the publisher in the first place.

278. Q. Does this mean that every time a book is reprinted the copyright begins again?

A. No. If the reprint is simply a reproduction of the original typographical arrangement, no new copyright comes into force.

279. Q. Supposing it is a new layout of the book?

A. Then copyright subsists *in that particular edition.*

280. Q. What if it is the same typesetting but a long new introduction has been written?

A. There will be a new copyright in the new introduction, owned originally by the author of that introduction. The publisher can claim copyright in the whole work (introduction and text) together, but the original text will only be a reproduction of an earlier text and is covered only for the time that typographical copyright lasts.

Example. Shakespeare is long out of copyright but a new edition of his works will go into copyright for 25 years to protect the typography. This does not stop someone else bringing out their own edition or photocopying older editions that are out of copyright.

281. Q. Does the existence of this separate copyright prevent libraries and others from copying materials as described earlier?

A. No. The law specifically states that anything that can be done by way of copying with a copyright work can also be done to the typographical layout of that work.

282. Q. What constitutes a new edition of an electronically-stored work?

A. That is difficult to decide. Obviously if a whole new piece is added then the work is a new edition but if, as in the case of a database, material is added frequently and in small pieces, it is difficult to say whether every addition creates a new edition or whether a lot of new data has to be added before this can be claimed. A further problem is that no actual printed version will be made every time a change is made so some editions may come and go and never be known about.

SECTION FIVE
Artistic works

Definition

282a. Q. What is the definition of an artistic work?
   A. The definition of artistic works includes:
   Graphic works such as paintings, drawings, diagrams, maps, charts and plans, engravings, lithographs, etchings or woodcuts;
   Sculpture;
   Collage;
   Photographs (including slides and negatives), architectural works (including buildings of any kind);
   Works of artistic craftsmanship such as jewellery or pottery.

283. Q. Does a slide count as a photograph?
   A. Yes. Slides are protected in the same way as photographs.

284. Q. Are overhead transparencies (OHPs) protected by copyright?
   A. Yes, they are another type of photograph.

Ownership of Copyright

285. Q. Who owns the copyright in an artistic work?
   A. Ownership of the copyright of an artistic work is defined in the same terms as for a literary, dramatic or musical work. (See questions 26ff).

Definition of Author

286. Q. Who counts as the author of an artistic work?
   A. The author of an artistic work is defined in the same terms as for a literary, dramatic or musical work. (See questions 32ff).

287. Q. Who owns the copyright in a collection of slides?

A. Each slide has its own copyright just like the articles in periodical (see question 40). However, there will also be a copyright in a compilation made up of slides.

Duration of copyright

288. Q. Is the length of copyright different for artistic works?

A. For works created after 1 August 1989 the term of copyright is the same as for other works, i.e. year of author's death + 50 years or publication + 50 years for anonymous works. However, there are some complex rules for works already in existence. Briefly, they are as follows:

Engravings

Published

Artist's death + 50 years

If published after artist's death and before 1 August 1989: year of publication + 50 years.

If anonymous: year of publication + 50 years

Unpublished

Unpublished and the artist died before 1 August 1989: protected until 31 December 2039.

Otherwise protected from year of artist's death + 50 years

Anonymous works: protected until 31 December 2039

Photographs

Because photographs enjoyed different protections under the different Copyright Acts, their position is particularly complicated. The table below gives the details:

Unpublished photographs

Taken before 1 June 1957: copyright lasts for 50 years from the end of the year in which the photograph was taken.

Taken 1 June 1957 to 31 July 1989: copyright expires on 31 December 2039

Taken on or after 1 August 1989 − author unknown: copyright is perpetual until published

Taken on or after 1 August 1989 − author known: copyight lasts for 50 years after the author's death.

Published photographs

Taken before 1 June 1957: copyright lasts for 50 years from the end of the year in which the photograph was taken.

Taken 1 June 1957 to 31 July 1989: copyright lasts for 50 years from the end of the year of publication.

Taken on or after 1 August 1989 - author known: copyright lasts for 50 years after the author's death.

Taken on or after 1 August 1989 - author unknown: copyright lasts for 50 years from year of publication.

Crown and Parliamentary Copyright

Artistic works are subject to Crown and Parliamentary Copyright in the same way as literary, dramatic or musical works (see questions 62ff).

Other artistic works

289. Q. When does the copyright in other artistic works expire?
     A. Fifty years after the year in which the author dies.

290. Q. What if these are anonymous?
     A. Then copyright expires 50 years after they are made available to the public.

291. Q. What constitutes 'available'?
     A. This includes public exhibition, including them in a film shown to the public or including them in a public broadcast. If none of these things has happpened, and the work is anonymous, copyright is perpetual.

Copying Artistic works

Owner's rights

The owner has the same rights as for literary, dramatic or musical works.

Copying the work

The owner has the exclusive right to make copies of the work.

292. Q. What about taking photographs?
     A. A photograph of an artistic work (say a statue or painting) is an infringement of the artist's copyright unless the work is on permanent public display in a public open space or premises open to the public.

293. Q. What constitutes 'open to the public'?
     A. This is not defined but it would certainly be a street or thoroughfare and any building to which the public had access

in the normal course of events. Presumably a library, museum or art gallery is open to the public although particular parts of it may not be, so these would not count (e.g. strong rooms, vaults, closed stacks, etc.). Rooms in Town Halls and other similar buildings are more difficult to define.

294. Q. The owners of some buildings charge copying fees to photograph artistic works housed in them even though the works must surely be out of copyright. Is this allowed?
     A. This is not a copyright fee but a copying fee. The owners of a Cathedral, for example, cannot claim there is copyright in a medieval painting but this does not stop them from charging for the privilege of access to photograph their property. The painting is their property even though the copyright has long since expired.

295. Q. What about making a slide, OHP or microform of a painting?
     A. Photocopying, microfilming or making a transparency or slide of a drawing, engraving or painting are all infringements.

296. Q. What about making a model of something in a painting?
     A. It is also an infringement to make a three-dimensional model of a picture, photograph or painting in just the same way as photographing a statue is an infringement.

297. Q. What constitutes 'permanent'?
     A. Unfortunately this is not defined. Obviously something on loan for, say, six months, could not be permanent. Something might be on display for six months and then taken away and be counted as permanent because it was intended to be so when it was put on display in the first place.

298. Q. What happens if a photograph (or television programme) happens to include a piece of copyright material in the background. Say an interview in front of a recent painting in a gallery?
     A. Incidental copying of this nature is not an infringement — but it would be if the photograph deliberately included the painting.

299. Q. Supposing the library/archive holds a painting which it wishes to reproduce as a slide, poster or postcard?

A. If the painting is out of copyright there is no problem or if the picture is of a statue or something similar on permanent public display then there is no problem. Remember the slide, poster or postcard will attract copyright which will be owned by the photographer or the library/archive depending on whether the photographer was an employee of the library/archive or the library/archive simply commissioned the taking of the photograph!

300. Q. Supposing there is an exhibition of children's work and the library wants to use this for publicity material or to publish it?

A. Technically the copyright belongs to the children individually and the permission of the child or guardian is necessary before works can be reproduced. Some teachers might argue that the copyright belongs to the school but the child is not employed there (at least not in the sense of gainful employment!) and the teacher cannot claim the copyright because the child actually did the painting.

Issue copies to the public

This is restricted as for literary, dramatic and musical works (see questions 78ff). Note that there is no rental right in artistic works.

Performing the work

There is no performing right for artistic works.

301. Q. Can the owner of a painting or other artistic work put it on public display?

A. Yes. The right of display is not one of the acts restricted by copyright. Once the work has been purchased the owner of the work may display it but this does not alter the rights of the copyright owner to reproduce the work, e.g. on postcards, photographs, slides etc.

Broadcast the work

6302. Q. Supposing a television programme included a shot of a painting or sculpture. Would this be counted as broadcasting?

A. Yes, unless it was incidentally included as mentioned in

61

question 298. However, if the programme were about a particular painter whose works were still in copyright then the inclusion would be deliberate and would infringe the artist's copyright.

303. Q. Supposing the television programme is a news item about an artist who has just died and that is being reported.
   A. Then, to include one of the artist's paintings as part of the news would not be an infringement because this would be reporting current events (see questions 117ff).

Adaptation

304. Q. Is there a right of adaptation in artistic works? How does it work?
   A. In theory there is but in practice this is copying. For example, to make a model of a painting is really an adaptation of the original to a different form as mentioned under 'models' (question 296).

Exceptions (allowances)

Fair dealing

305. Q. Are artistic works subject to fair dealing?
   A. Artistic works are subject to fair dealing in a similar way to literary, dramatic and musical works but there are some differences.

306. Q. What constitutes fair dealing in an artistic work?
   A. This is undefined as for other works. However, the same general rules apply (see questions 97ff).

307. Q. Do the reasons for fair dealing − research or private study; criticism or review and reporting current events − still apply to artistic works?
   A. Yes. The reasons are just the same except in the area of reporting current events.

Research or private study

308. Q. Can artistic works be copied for research or private study?
   A. Yes, like literary works.

309. Q. How can something be copied fairly when it is an artistic work? Surely the whole of the work would be copied?

A. Perhaps. Fair dealing does not exclude copying all of the work.

Example. An art student needs to study the different ways of portraying Hercules. The student could take photographs of modern statues, paintings and drawings for personal use to carry out the research. The photographs must not be sold or published or they would not constitute fair dealing for the purposes of research. If they were subsequently sold or published this would be an infringement.

310. Q. What about people who go to art galleries (and libraries) and make paintings of other people's paintings?

A. This would be considered as fair because it is for private study. In any case the copy would have had sufficient original input from the copying painter to qualify for copyright protection in its own right.

311. Q. Can a student include a copy of an artistic work, say a photograph of a statue, in a thesis?

A. Yes. This is for research and also providing the answer to an examination, so it is covered by educational copying. But if the thesis is published then the copyright in the artistic work is infringed.

Reporting current events

312. Q. Can artistic works be used to report current events?

A. Yes but photographs may not be used for this purpose. See the general section on 'criticism and review' (questions 117ff).

Criticism or review

Artistic works may be reproduced for criticism or review provided that there is sufficient acknowledgement of their authorship.

313. Q. What constitutes sufficient acknowledgement?

A. This is not defined but would presumably include the name of the author at least.

314. Q. Can an artistic work be reproduced in a journal article?
     A. Only if the purpose is criticism or review. Simply to include a photograph of a copyright painting to illustrate a point about modern art would not be sufficient justification.

315. Q. What about using a painting or photograph of a piece of sculpture to advertise an exhibition?
     A. This would not be allowed.

316. Q. What about sale catalogues which include photographs of copyright materials?
     A. That is allowed. There is a specific clause allowing the copying of works to advertise them for sale.

Educational copying

317. Q. May artistic works be copied for educational purposes?
     A. Artistic works may be copied by either the teacher or the pupil themselves so long as a reprographic process is not used.
        Example. A teacher or student could make their own copy of a map by drawing it themselves but must not photocopy it.

318. Q. What about examination questions?
     A. Anything may be done for setting questions or answering them so there are no restrictions in this area.

319. Q. What about educational licensing schemes?
     A. The schemes described under literary works do not extend to artistic works nor does the Copyright Act make provision for them to do so but other schemes may well be available. It is advisable to check.

320. Q. What is to be done for the classroom teacher who wants multiple copies of, say, a photograph, for classroom use?
     A. This is not permitted. However, each student is allowed to make their own copy for research or private study purposes.

321. Q. Can slides or photographs be made of artistic works for classroom use or teaching?
     A. Not without infringing copyright.

322. Q. Can a slide be included in, say, a film or video?
     A. No. That is copying just like any other form of copying.

323. Q. Can an OHP be made of a work for classroom use?
     A. Not without infringing the copyright.

324. Q. Can copies be made of maps for classroom use?
     A. Photocopies for classsroom use cannot be made except under the licence of the copyright owner. Teachers and pupils may copy maps out of atlases by hand or through tracing paper as this is not a reprographic process

Library and archive copying

325. Q. Can libraries and archives copy artistic works in their collections in the same way as printed materials?
     A. No. The special provisions for library and archive copying do not apply to artistic works.

326. Q. What is to be done for a reader who wants a copy of a photograph?
     A. The reader may borrow the item and copy it for himself but the librarian is not allowed to copy on behalf of the reader.

327. Q. What about copying maps for users?
     A. Under copyright law this is not permitted. Users may make their own copies under fair dealing arrangements.

328. Q. What about licences issued by publishers such as Ordnance Survey?
     A. These are really a contract between the library and the copyright owner who is allowing the library to do certain things the law does not. As owners of the copyright Ordnance Survey (or any other publisher) are entitled to do anything they wish with their property! Failure to observe the conditions of such a licence is a breach of contract as well as an infringement of copyright.

329. Q. Supposing an article in a periodical is accompanied by a photograph?
     A. This can safely be copied as the act makes it clear that accompanying materials can legitimately be copied, whether or not they are artistic works as such.

330. Q. Are libraries allowed to supply copies of artistic works through interlibrary copying?
A. No.

331. Q. What if a library or archive has lost its copy of an artistic work. Can a replacement be obtained from another library or archive?
A. No. Copying for preservation or replacement is restricted to literary, dramatic or musical works.

Copying as a condition of export

331a. Q. Can artistic works be copied as condition of export?
A. Like literary work, an article of cultural or historical importance may be copied if a condition of the export is that a copy be made and deposited in an appropriate library or archive.

Material open for public inspection

No specific mention is made of material open to public inspection of artistic works. However see this section under literary, dramatic or musical work for references to maps.

Public administration

The same wide allowances apply to artistic works as to literary works.

SECTION SIX

Sound recordings

331*b*. Q. What is the definition of a sound recording?

A. The definition of a sound recording is not limited in any way by format. It is any form of recording of sounds from which sounds may be reproduced. So it includes wax cylinders, vinyl discs, audio cassettes, compact discs and digital audio tape. It also includes sounds recorded and stored in digital form from which sounds can be reproduced.

Authorship

332. Q. Who is the author of a sound recording?

A. The author of a sound recording is the person who made the arrangements for making the recording.

333. Q. Does this mean that a record company owns the copyright in the songs of the artists who make recordings for it?

A. No. It is very important to distinguish between the copyright in the sound recording and the copyright in the material recorded.

Examples. A recording of a song by the Beatles will have all sorts of copyrights − the the song, the music, the arrangement and the performance. In addition, there is a copyright in the actual sound recording which is quite separate. Similarly, an interview for an oral history project will have a copyright in what the person said which will belong to the person interviewed. There will also be a copyright in the recording made of that inverview which will be owned by the person who made the arrangements for making the recording. Again, a recording of Beethoven's Fifth Symphony will have a copyright in the recording although there is no longer any copyright in the music as such.

[NB. This is important outside libraries as the law now says it is not an infringement of the copyright in a sound recording to play it in organizations such as youth clubs. This applies only to the recording and not to the music or words of the recording.]

Duration of copyright

334. Q. Is the length of copyright linked to the lives of some or all of the artists?
     A. No. The rules are different.

335. Q. How long does copyright in a sound recording last?
     A. Complicated, rather like photographs. Again, the table below gives the details:
        Unpublished
        Made before 1 June 1957: copyright lasts from the year it was made + 50 years
        Made on or after 1 June 1957 and before 1 August, 1989: copyright lasts until 31 December 2039
        Made on or after 1 August 1989: copyright lasts for 50 years from the year it was made.
        Published (or released)
        Made before 1 June 1957: copyright lasts from the year it was made + 50 years
        Made on or after 1 June 1957: copyright lasts for 50 years from the year of publication

336. Q. Does 'released' mean published?
     A. Not quite. Released means published in the usual sense but also if the sound recording is included in a broadcast or cable television programme. This is important for sound archive material which is lent to broadcasting organizations. The transmission of the material will mean it has been published or released and the copyright in it will expire 50 years from that time rather than 50 years from when it was made.

Copying sound recordings

Owner's rights

The owner has the same rights as for literary, dramatic, musical or artistic works.

Copy the work

The owner has the exclusive right to make copies of the work.

337. Q. Does this include copying from one medium to another?
    A. Yes. To make a copy of a vinyl disc onto a tape is, of course, copying the work.

338. Q. Supposing the medium on which the work is stored is obsolete? Can copies be made onto a usable type of equipment.
    A. Not without permission or infringing copyright.

Issue copies to the public

This is an exclusive right of the owner

339. Q. If this right includes rental, does this mean that lending services for audio materials are not allowed?
    A. Basically, yes. Sound recordings may not be rented (or loaned) to the public without the copyright owner's permission.

340. Q. Does this mean that libraries may no longer lend records?
    A. Not altogether. In the first place, this restriction applies only to material acquired on or after 1 August 1989. Secondly, there may well be special agreements with the production industries to allow rental or lending facilities under agreed terms. It is best to check either the conditions of purchase of particular materials in the library or seek advice on the latest situation from the Library Association (see appendix of useful addresses). Thirdly, it is made clear that even free loan is prohibited in the case of public libraries although other libraries may be able to make free loans. This last possibility depends on the interpretation of the word 'rental'. If this means lending for payment then any library (other than a public library) can lend audiovisual materials without a licence but if it means lending whether for money or not then no library can offer a lending service for these materials without a licence.

341. Q. Why are public libraries excluded?
    A. Because the Act specifically states that the rental right is exclusive to the copyright owner including lending by public libraries whether or not a charge is made for the facility.

342. Q. Supposing there is no licensing scheme available?
    A. The Secretary of State has the power to implement a scheme subject to appropriate payment as determined by the Copyright Tribunal if necessary.

343. Q. Supposing a work is held by a library in both printed form and as, say, an audiocassette. What is the position then?
    A. This causes an anomaly. The printed book is subject to Public Lending Right but the audiocassette is controlled by the licensing scheme offered by the producers of audio materials, probably through the BPI (British Phonographic Industry's) licence. There is a further anomaly, in that the money for the Public Lending Right royalty comes from the government and goes to the author; any money from the audio licensing scheme (if there is one) is paid by the library and goes to the producer of the cassette.

Perform the work

The owner has the exclusive right to perform the work.

344. Q. Does this mean that if a library has a collection of sound recordings and wishes to put on a public performance of them, this is not allowed?
    A. This can be done either with non-copyright material (i.e. it is too old to be protected) or with material in which the library or archive holds the copyright or if the library is covered by a Performing Rights Licence.

345. Q. Who owns the copyright in an interview?
    A. This is important for oral history and similar archives. The speaker owns the copyright in what is said but there is no copyright in the material until it hs been recorded. Once it has been recorded the speaker owns the copyright in what has been said but the person making the recording owns the copyright in the sound recording as such.

346. Q. Is it necessary to get permission to make such recordings for archives?

A. It is advisable to obtain the permission of the speaker when the recording is made. Such permission should stipulate for what purposes the recording will be used, especially if it may be used later by a radio programme or television station.

347. Q. Supposing the library or archive holds oral history recordings. Can these be played publicly?

A. Only if the library/archive owns the copyright in both the words spoken and the sound recording itself.

348. Q. How can the library or archive obtain the copyright in the actual words spoken?

A. This is best done by way of an agreement with the interviewee at the time of the interview. Failure to do this could lead to infringement of the speaker's copyright.

349. Q. If the library has a collection of sound recordings, can they be played on the library's premises?

A. They can be played for private listening in carrels or somewhere similar. Otherwise they can be played only if the library (or the library authority) has a Performing Rights Act licence which covers that building. Otherwise, public playing of copyright material is an infringement. Check with the library administration to see if the library is covered by such a licence. This also applies to films, videos, television broadcasts and radio.

Broadcast the work

350. Q. Presumably libraries and archives do not have to worry about restrictions on broadcasting?

A. Not true. There is an increasing interest in local studies and live comments from the past, as well as folk music and recent broadcast interviews. Where this material has been prepared, recorded or given to the library or archive, it may well be in demand from local or national broadcasting stations. To allow this to be used in this way is an infringement unless the original owner gave express permission when the recording was made.

71

Adaptation

This is an exclusive right of the owner

Exceptions (allowances)

Fair dealing

351. Q. Is there fair dealing in sound recordings?
     A. Only for very restricted purposes. See the individual headings below.

Research or private study

There is no fair dealing in sound recordings for the purposes of research or private study.

352. Q. What can be done for a student who needs a copy of a sound recording for study purposes?
     A. There is no legal way that such a copy can be provided. The only thing to do is to obtain permission from the copyright owner.

Reporting current events

353. Q. Can sound recordings be used for reporting current events?
     A. Yes. Short extracts from appropriate recordings can be used for new items and there is no need to acknowledge their source.

Criticism and review

354. Q. Can sound recordings be used for criticism or review?
     A. Yes, so long as the source is acknowledged. So a broadcast which includes short extracts from sound recordings to provide comment on the work of a singer or composer is allowed.

Library and archive copying

355. Q. Can libraries and archives copy sound recordings?
     A. No. The provisions for copying in libraries and archives are for literary, dramatic and musical works only.

356. Q. Can a library or archive copy sound recordings for preservation purposes?
A. Unfortunately, no. Again, these allowances are for literary, dramatic or musical works only.

356a. Q. What can be done if a record or tape is deteriorating rapidly and will be lost if it is not copied?
A. Legally, nothing if it is still in copyright. If the owner can be traced, permission can be sought but otherwise the library or archive may take a risk and produce a substitute copy. It is a matter of fine judgement whether the original copyright owner would take action if this were discovered.

357. Q. What happens if someone wishes to record a folksong for an archive?
A. There are special rules for this. In the first place the song must be of unknown authorship *and* be unpublished. In other words, a real original folksong. If this really is the case then a recording can be made, so long as the performer does not prohibit this.

358. Q. Can the recording be kept in any local history archive?
A. Not initially. Only certain designated archives can maintain collections of these items.

359. Q. Which archives are these?
A. There are quite a number of them but they are all national in character. There is a complete list in SI 89/1012, at the end of this book.

360. Q. Can copies be made from these recordings?
A. Yes, provided that the archivist is satisfied that they are for research or private study only and not more than one copy is supplied to any one person.

361. Q. Is there the usual requirement that they must be paid for?
A. Surprisingly, no. No mention is made of payment.

362. Q. Can archives keep off-air recordings made for 'time-shifting' purposes?
A. No. These copies should not be kept for long periods even by the individual who made them. Given that they are often

73

kept and this cannot be monitored in the home, it certainly can be monitored in a publicly-accessible place such as an archive and such copies must not be kept.

363. Q. Supposing someone's papers are deposited with an archive and these papers include copies of audiovisual materials such as off-air recordings. Can the archive keep these?

       A. In theory, no. They are infringing copies because off-air recording can be done only for certain limited purposes and storing the copies in an archive is not one of them.

364. Q. Can a library or archive copy off-air to keep a relevant programme in its collection?

       A. No. Some archives have special arrangements with broadcasting bodies to make off-air recordings for archival purposes but these are specific to each archive.

365. Q. Can they make copies for other archives?

       A. Not under copyright law. They may have other agreements with production companies which allow this.

Educational copying

366. Q. Is there any way that libraries and schools can record off-air for future use?

       A. Yes for some programmes. The law allows off-air recording for educational use if there is no licensing scheme. However, schemes covering most broadcast materials are available so this type of off-air recording should not cause too many problems, but it is important to check the terms of any licence held.

367. Q. Do these schemes cover all that teachers require?

       A. Yes, usually they do. Anything for which there is no licence may be copied until a licence for that material is offered.

368. Q. Supposing the terms of the licence are such that a school or college does not wish to take it out?

       A. They can either complain to the Copyright Tribunal that the terms of the licence are unfair or they can decline to join the licensing scheme at all and forfeit any right to record off-air under that licence.

Copying as a condition of export

369. Q. Do the special arrangements for copying materials of historic or cultural importance before export apply to sound recordings?

A. Yes. If the condition of export is that a copy is made and deposited in a library or archive, then this is not an infringement and the library or archive can make the copy, or receive the copy made elsewhere.

Material open to public inspection

370. Q. Do the special conditions about copying such material apply to sound recordings?

A. It is not very likely that this would arise but the appropriate person may make copies either for use by persons who cannot exercise their statutory rights by consulting the material in person or if the material contains information of general scientific, technical, commercial or economic interest. Copies may not be made for persons consulting it in person.

Public Administration

371. Q. Can sound recordings be copied for judicial proceedings, parliamentary proceedings and statutory inquiries, as in the case of literary works?

A. Yes. There is no restriction in this case.

SECTION SEVEN

Films and videos

Definition

371a. Q. What is the definition of a film?
  A. The definition of a film includes anything from which a moving image can be produced. This covers video, videodisc, optical disc and any other new technologies which produce moving images.

Authorship

372. Q. Who is the author of a film?
  A. The same as sound recordings, the person making the arrangements for making the film. Remember that it is the film of which the person making the arrangement owns the copyright, not the content.
  Example. A television programme includes an interview with a song writer, several performances of his songs and an extract of a film containing a performance of his songs. The song-writer will own the copyright in his words in the interview and the words and music of his songs; the person making the TV programme will own the copyright in the programme as a whole and the film maker will own the copyright in the extract of the film included in the programme.

Duration of copyright

373. Q. Is the length of copyright linked to the life of a particular person?
  A. No. The rules are different, as in sound recordings.

374. Q. How long does the copyright in a film last?
    A. Rather like photographs and sound recordings, this is not a simple question to asnwer. Basically the rules are as follows:
    Released films
    Made before 1 June 1957: no copyright exists in the film as such but it is treated as an original dramatic work instead.
    Films made on or after 1 June 1957: copyright lasts for 50 years from the end of the year of first release.
    Unreleased films
    Made before 1 June 1957: no copyright exists in the film as such but it is treated as an original dramatic work instead.
    Made 1 June 1957 to 31 July 1989: copyright lasts until 31 December 2039.
    Films made after 1 August 1989: copyright lasts for 50 years from the end of the year in which it was made.
    Copying films
    Owner's rights
    Like all copyright materials, the owner has certain exclusive rights.
    Copying the work
    Copying the work is the owner's exclusive right.

375. Q. Does this include transferring from one medium to another?
    A. Yes. Copying a film onto a video is copying just as disc to tape is copying for sound recordings.

376. Q. Supposing the medium on which the work is stored is obsolete? Can copies be made onto a usable type of equipment?
    A. Not without permission or infringing copyright.

377. Q. Are archives allowed to copy films for preservation as they can for literary works?
    A. No. The allowances for archival and replacement copying are for literary, dramatic and musical works only. They do not apply to films.

Issue copies to the public

This is an exclusive right of the owner.

77

378. Q. If this right includes rental, does this mean that lending services for video materials are not allowed?
A. Basically, yes. Videos (and films) may not be rented (or loaned) to the public without the copyright owner's permission.

379. Q. Does this mean that libraries may no longer lend videos?
A. Not altogether. In the first place, this restriction applies only to material acquired on or after 1 August 1989. Secondly, there may well be special agreements with the production industries to allow rental/lending facilities under agreed terms. It is best to check either the conditions of purchase of particular materials in the library or seek advice on the latest situation from the Library Association (see appendix of useful addresses). Thirdly, it is made clear that even free loan is prohibited in the case of public libraries although other libraries may be able to make free loans. This last possibility depends on the interpretation of the word 'rental'. If this means lending for payment then any library (other than a public library) can lend audiovisual materials without a licence but if it means lending whether for money or not then no library can offer a lending service for these materials without a licence.

380. Q. Why are public libraries excluded?
A. Because the Act specifically states that the rental right is exclusive to the copyright owner including lending by public libraries whether or not a charge is made for the facility.

381. Q. Supposing there is no rental scheme available?
A. The Secretary of State has the power to implement a scheme subject to appropriate payment as determined by the Copyright Tribunal if necessary.

Perform the work

The owner has the exclusive right to perform the work. For other matters relating to performance of a work see this heading under 'Sound recordings' as the same basic rules apply and the same problems arise.

Broadcast the work

See this heading under 'Sound recordings'.

Adaptation

The owner has the exclusive right to adapt the work.

Exceptions (allowances)

381*a*. Q.   Is there fair dealing in films?

Fair dealing

There is no fair dealing in film or videos except for the specific cases mentioned below.

Research or private study

There is no fair dealing in films or videos for research or private study.

Reporting current events

See this heading under 'Sound recordings'.

Criticism and review

See this heading under 'Sound recordings'.

Library and archive copying

382.   Q.   Can libraries or archives copy films or videos in their collections?

    A.   In general, no. The special provisions for library and archive copying apply only to literary, dramatic or musical works but not to other works.

383.   Q.   What is to be done for a researcher who needs a copy of part of a film or video?

    A.   The copy cannot be supplied unless the copyright in the material is owned by the library or archive or the original copyright owner has given permission for copies to be made.

384.   Q.   Can a library or archive copy off-air to keep a relevant programme in its collection?

    A.   No. The law allows the Secretary of State to designate archives which may make off-air recordings for archival purposes. No other archive may do so (see question 398).

385. Q. Can they make copies for other archives?
A. Not under copyright law. They may have other agreements with production companies which allow this.

386. Q. What about copies of recordings made for 'time-shifting'?
A. These should not be kept. See question 418.

Educational copying

387. Q. Can films to copied for classroom use?
A. No. The only exception is for training in the making of films or film sound-tracks and then only by the teacher or pupil themselves. But they can be played or viewed by the class as they are broadcast.

Copying as a condition of export

See this heading under 'Sound recordings'.

Material open to public inspection

See this heading under 'Sound recordings'.

Public Administration

See this heading under 'Sound Recordings'.

Microforms

388. Q. Do microforms qualify for copyright?
A. Certainly. A microfilm or microfiche ('microforms' for short) is a photograph and attracts copyright in the same way as a photograph itself.

389. Q. How long is a microform protected then?
A. If the author can be established, for 50 years from the year of the author's death; otherwise 50 years from the year in which the microform was made available to the public.

390. Q. What happens if the work which has been microfilmed is still in copyright?
A. There are then two copyrights, one in the original document and one in the microform. To do this would require the consent of the original copyright owner.

391. Q. Supposing the work that has been microfilmed is out of copyright?
A. There is still copyright in the microform as a photograph even though the work photographed is out of copyright.

392. Q. What is the situation if enlargements are made from the microform?
A. The enlargements can be an infringement of microform and the original document, if the original is still in copyright, or of just the microform if that is still in copyright but the document filmed is not.
Example. A microform of Magna Carta would attract copyright as a photograph but the Magna Carta certainly would not.

393. Q. Supposing a library wishes to make microform copies of works in its collection to preserve them?
A. This is in order only if the original documents are out of copyright or if they come under the special provisions for preservation (see questions 234ff).

394. Q. If a library or archive makes its own microforms, who owns the copyright?
A. The copyright belongs to the library or archive.

Mixed-media

395. Q. If a publication contains material in several different forms such as a booklet, computer program and video, how is the copyright worked out?
A. The copyright will subsist separately in each item and the rules for that format will apply. So the copyright in the entire package could run out at several different times. In that sense, it is no different from a periodical issue.

395a. Q. Who is the author of a mixed-media package?
A. The rules for ownership and authorship are the same as for each of the components. However, the publisher may also place a blanket claim on copyright in the format of the whole package.

SECTION EIGHT

Broadcasts

Most matters relating to broadcasts, from a library and archive point of view, are dealt with under either 'sound recordings' or 'films'.

Definition

396. Q. What is the definition of a broadcast?
   A. The definition of a broadcast includes wireless, television, cable and satellite transmission.

397. Q. What about a broadcast which includes a record, like most Radio One programmes?
   A. There are separate copyrights in the broadcast and the sound recording included in it. In the same way a television programme which includes a film has separate copyrights in the television transmission and the film in the programme.

398. Q. Can a library or archive copy off-air to keep a relevant programme in its collection?
   A. No. Only designated archives are entitled to copy off-air for archival purposes. Only four archives have been designated for the purposes of making off-air recordings for archival purposes. These are the National Film Archive, the British Library (intended for the National Sound Archive but this is not specified), the Scottish Film Archive and the Music Performance Research Centre.

398a. Q. Is off-air recording allowed at all?
   A. It is an infringement to copy broadcasts, except for time shifting purposes (see question 418), and it is also an infringement to take a photograph of a film except for private or domestic use. There are exceptions for educational copying (see question 387).

Definition of authorship

399. Q. Who is the author of a broadcast?
     A. The person responsible for transmitting the broadcast. (But see also questions 332ff).

Duration

400. Q. When does the copyright in a broadcast expire?
     A. Copyright in a broadcast expires 50 years after the year when the broadcast was made.

401. Q. What about repeats?
     A. The fact that a programme was repeated does not extend or renew the copyright. However, no copyright exists in any broadcast made before 1 June 1957. But beware! Copyright may well still exist in the content of the broadcast.

Educational copying

402. Q. Can broadcasts be copied for classroom use, too?
     A. Only with the appropriate licence and such licences are now generally available for education establishments. One exception is for training in the making of films or film sound-tracks and then only by the teacher or pupil themselves. But they can be played or viewed by the class as they are broadcast.

SECTION NINE

Other matters

Licensing schemes

403. Q. What is a licensing scheme?
     A. Basically it is a scheme which allows someone, who is not the copyright owner, to use copyright material beyond the limits of the law.

404. Q. Who administers such schemes?
     A. They are administered by different organizations and these can change. One or two useful addresses of schemes in existence at the time this book was written (1989) are given in the list of useful addresses at the end.

405. Q. Are licensing schemes relevant to libraries?
     A. Certainly. Firstly, because any licence held by the organization which owns or administers the library will almost certainly include copying done in the library. Secondly, because in the case of sound recordings, films and videos and computer software a licence may be the only way the library can offer a lending service for these materials.

406. Q. Do libraries have to abide by the rules of such licences?
     A. Yes. They represent a contract between the licensing agency and the licensee.

407. Q. What are the details of such schemes?
     A. Each scheme will vary according to the type of material covered and the type of organization handling the licence. No specific guidance can be given but it is very important that all librarians should know if their organization holds such a licence and what the terms of that licence are. This can

alter the type of services offered, either limiting it, or, quite often, allowing it to expand beyond what would appear allowable under the law.

408. Q. What is the difference between a licensing scheme and a licence?

A. Nobody is entirely certain of the nicer points of this at present but basically a licensing scheme is generally available to anyone who wants to take it up and is advertised at a fixed scale of charges. Licences are individually tailored and are negotiated according to individual circumstances and are not therefore generally offered. Licensing schemes are subject to the rulings of the Copyright Tribunal but licences may not be.

409. Q. Many journals have details of payment to the Copyright Clearance Center in the USA printed on the bottom of the page. Must libraries pay these fees to CCC?

A. Payment should be made only if copying is done beyond what UK law permits. The Copyright Licensing Agency (CLA) currently acts as the agent for the CCC and they should be contacted in cases of doubt. See the list of useful addresses at the end of the book.

International copyright

410. Q. What importance does international copyright have?

A. Technically there is no such thing as 'international copyright'. Each country has its own copyright laws but most major countries belong to either or both of the international conventions. Under these treaties and conventions each country protects the works produced in other countries as if they had been produced within its own borders, although usually works are not protected in a country for longer than they would be in the country of origin. So if a work is produced in a country where protection lasts for 50 yers but is imported into a country where protection lasts for 70 years, then the work would still be protected for only 50 years in that country.

411. Q. Which are these two major conventions?

A. The Berne Copyright Convention and the Universal Copyright Convention.

412. Q. Are there any countries which do not belong to any of these conventions?

A. Yes. Many smaller countries do not belong to either convention (although equally many small countries do), but important countries which do not belong (as of 1989) are China, Saudi Arabia and Malaysia.

413. Q. Does this mean that their publications can be copied?

A. Yes, without restriction. It also means that British publications can be freely copied in those countries which deters many exporters from sending their publications there.

414. Q. What is the importance of the Copyright Symbol ©?

A. The idea of the symbol is to indicate the work was protected by copyright in the country of origin and had been registered for copyright protection. This is important under the Universal Copyright Convention as publications without the symbol are not regarded as protected. As the USA has now joined the Berne convention, under which no formality is required for registering a copyright document, the symbol is chiefly important on publications from those countries which belong to the UCC but not to Berne. It also protects publications in those same UCC countries, so it is important for publishers to include it on their works even if it is not required in the country of origin as it should protect them when exported to UCC countries. The main producer of literary works in this category is currently the USSR although it is thought that the USSR will join the Berne Convention soon.

Legal deposit

415. Q. What is the connection between copyright deposit and copyright law?

A. None, nor has there been for many years. Copyright deposit is there to enable the national libraries to build up collections of the national printed archive.

416. Q. Why is it called copyright deposit?

A. Because it used to be a prerequisite for being able to claim copyright. But international conventions require that no formality is necessary before claiming copyright. Really copyright deposit should now be called 'legal deposit'.

Public Lending Right

417. Q. Is there a connection between copyright and Public Lending Right?
     A. Not directly and certainly not in law. In many countries PLR is part of copyright legislation but in the UK is is quite separate. The connection is that the original copyright owner (the author) receives payment under PLR; the publisher does not. So for this purpose the identity of the original author is important; PLR also continues to be paid for the duration of copyright so that there is a further link there. The funds for PLR come from the government whereas those for licensing schemes come from those using the copyright materials covered by that licence.

418 Q. Is recording off-air allowed at home?
     A. Yes. Recordings from broadcasts may be made for private and domestic use only. Copies may not be kept for long periods nor can they be used for other purposes such as classroom use or archival collections.

Definitions

The Act defines some terms precisely but not others. A list of the more important definitions for librarians and archivists contained in the Act is given at the end of this book.

APPENDIX 1

List of useful addresses

The Library Association
7 Ridgmount Street
London WC1E 7AE

The Copyright Licensing Agency
33-34 Alfred Place
London WC1E 7DP

British Copyright Council
29 Berners Street
London W1P 4AA

Public Lending Right Office
Bayheath House
Prince Regent Street
Stockton-on-Tees
Cleveland
TS18 1DF

Educational Recording Agency
c/o Authors' Licensing and
   Collecting Society
Third Floor
7 Ridgmount Street
London WC1E 7AE

Education Copyright Users'
   Forum
c/o National Council for
   Educational Technology
3 Devonshire Street
London W1N 2BA

HMSO Copyright Section
St Crispins
Duke Street
Norwich NR1 1PO

Copyright Branch
Ordnance Survey
Romsey Road
Maybush
Southampton SO9 4DH

Hydrographic Department
Finance Section
Ministry of Defence
Taunton
Somerset TA1 2DN

APPENDIX 2

Some useful books and journals

Flint, Michael, Thorne, Clive D. and Williams, Alan P., *Intellectual property – the new law: a guide to the Copyright, Designs and Patents Act 1988*. London, Butterworths, 1989. ISBN 0 406 503079.

Merkin, Robert, *Richards Butler on Copyright, Designs and Patents: the new law*. London, Longman, 1989. ISBN 0 85121 565 3.

Dworkin, Gerald and Taylor, Richard D., *Blackstone's guide to the Copyright, Designs and Patents Act 1988: the law of copyright and related rights*. London, Blackstone Press, 1989. ISBN 0 85431 023 2.

Stewart, Stephen M., *International copyright and neighbouring rights*. Second edition. London, Butterworths, 1989. ISBN 0 406 66222 3.

Lester, David and Mitchell, Paul, *Joynson-Hicks on UK copyright law*. London, Sweet & Maxwell, 1989. ISBN 0 421 40960 6.

Copyright Bulletin. Published quarterly by Unesco, Paris.

Copyright. Monthly. Published by the World Intellectual Property Organization, Geneva.

European Intellectual Property Review. Published monthly by ESC Publishing, Oxford.

APPENDIX 3

Extracts from the legislation

Selected sections from the Copyright, Designs and Patents Act 1988

SI 89/1212. Copyright (Librarians and Archivists) (Copying of Copyright Materials) Order.

SI 89/1068 Copyright (Educational Establishments) (No.2) Order.

Selected sections from the Copyright, Designs and Patents Act 1988

General

29. (1) Fair dealing with a literary, dramatic, musical or artistic work for the purposes of research or private study does not infringe any copyright in the work or, in the case of a published edition, in the typographical arrangement.

    (2) Fair dealing with the typographical arrangement of a published edition for the purposes mentioned in subsection (1) does not infringe any copyright in the arrangement.

    (3) Copying by a person other than the researcher or student himself is not fair dealing if:

    (a) in the case of a librarian, or a person acting on behalf of a librarian, he does anything which regulations under section 40 would not permit to be under section 38 or 39 (articles or parts of published works: restriction on multiple copies of same material), or

    (b) in any other case, the person doing the copying knows or has reason to believe that it will result in copies of substantially the same material being provided to more than one person at substantially the same time and for substantially the same purpose.

Libraries and archives

37. (1) In sections 38 to 43 (copying by librarians and archivists):

    (a) references in any provision to a prescribed library or archive are to a library or archive of a description prescribed for the purposes of that provision by regulations made by the Secretary of State; and

    (b) references in any provision to the prescribed conditions are to the conditions so prescribed.

    (2) The regulations may provide that, where a librarian or archivist is required to be satisfied as to any matter before making or supplying a copy of a work:

    (a) he may relay on a signed declaration as to that matter by the person requesting the copy, unless he is aware that it is false in a material particular, and

    (b) in such cases as may be prescribed, he shall not make or supply a copy in the absence of a signed declaration in such form as may be prescribed.

(3) Where a person requesting a copy makes a declaration which is false in a material particular and is supplied with a copy which would have been an infringing copy if made by him:

(a) he is liable for infringement of copyright as if he had made the copy himself, and

(b) the copy shall be treated as an infringing copy.

(4) The regulations may make different provision for different descriptions of libraries or archives and for different purposes.

(5) Regulations shall be made by statutory instrument which shall be subject to annulment in pursuance of a resolution of either House of Parliament.

(6) References in this section, and in sections 38 to 43, to the librarian or archivist include a person acting on his behalf.

38. (1) The librarian of a prescribed library may, if the prescribed conditions are complied with, make and supply a copy of an article in a periodical without infringing any copyright in the text, in any illustrations accompanying the text or in the typographical arrangement.

(2) The prescribed conditions shall include the following:

(a) that copies are supplied only to persons satisfying the librarian that they require them for purposes of research or private study, and will not use them for any other purpose.

(b) that no person is furnished with more than one copy of the same article or with copies of more than one article contained in the same issue of a periodical; and

(c) that persons to whom copies are supplied are required to pay for them a sum not less than the cost (including a contribution to the general expenses of the library) attributable to their production.

39. (1) The librarian of a prescribed library may, if the prescribed conditions are complied with, make and supply from a published edition a copy of part of a literary, dramatic or musical work (other than an article in a periodical) without infringing any copyright in the work, in any illustrations accompanying the work or in the typographical arrangement.

(2) The prescribed conditions shall include the following:

(a) that copies are supplied only to persons satisfying the librarian that they require them for purposes of research or private study, and will not use them for any other purpose;

92

(b) that no person is furnished with more than one copy of the same material or with a copy of more than a reasonable proportion of any work; and

(c) that persons to whom copies are supplied are required to pay for them a sum not less than the cost (including a contribution to the general expenses of the library) attributable to their production.

40. (1) Regulations for the purposes of sections 38 and 39 (copying by librarian of article or part of published work) shall contain provision to the effect that a copy shall be supplied only to a person satisfying the librarian that his requirement is not related to any similar requirement of another person.

(2) The regulations may provide:

(a) that requirements shall be regarded as similar if the requirements are for copies of substantially the same material at substantially the same time and for substantially the same purpose; and

(b) that requirements of persons shall be regarded as related if those persons receive instruction to which the material is relevant at the same time and place.

41. (1) The librarian of a prescribed library may, if the prescribed conditions are complied with, make and supply to another prescribed library a copy of:

(a) an article in a periodical, or

(b) the whole or part of a published edition of a literary, dramatic or musical work,

without infringing any copyright in the text of the article or, as the case may be, in the work, in any illustrations accompanying it or in the typographical arrangement.

(2) Subsection (1)(b) does not apply if at the time the copy is made the librarian making it knows, or could be reasonable inquiry ascertain, the name and address of a person entitled to authorise the making of the copy.

42. (1) The librarian or archivist of a prescribed library or archive may, if the prescribed conditions are complied with, make a copy from any item in the permanent collection of the library or archive.

(a) in order to preserve or replace that item by placing the copy in its permanent collection in addition to or in place of it, or

(b) in order to replace in the permanent collection of another prescribed library or archive an item which has been lost, destroyed or damaged,

without infringing the copyright in any literary, dramatic or musical work, in any illustrations accompanying such a work or, in the case of a published edition, in the typographical arrangement.

(2)   The prescribed conditions shall include provision for restricting the making of copies to cases where it is not reasonably practicable to purchase a copy of the item in question to fulfil that purpose.

43.   (1)   The librarian or archivist of a prescribed library or archive may, if the prescribed conditions are complied with, make and supply a copy of the whole or part of a literary, dramatic or musical work from a document in the library or archive without infringing any copyright in the work or any illustrations accompanying it.

(2)   This section does not apply if:

(a)   the work had been published before the document was deposited in the library or archive, or

(b)   the copyright owner has prohibited copying of the work, and at the same time the copy is made the librarian or archivist making it is, or ought to be, aware of the fact.

(3)   The prescribed conditions shall include the following:

(a)   that copies are supplied only to persons satisfying the librarian or archivist that they require them for purposes of research or private study and will not use them for any other purpose;

(b)   that no person is furnished with more than one copy of the same material; and

(c)   that persons to whom copies are supplied are required to pay for them a sum not less than the cost (including a contribution to the general expenses of the library or archive) attributable to their production.

60.   (1)   Where an article on a scientific or technical subject is published in a periodical accompanied by an abstract indicating the contents of the article, it is not an infringement of copyright in the abstract, or in the article, to copy the abstract or issue copies of it to the public.

(2)   This section does not apply if or to the extent that there is a licensing scheme certified for the purposes of this section under section 143 providing for the grant of licences.

75. (1) A recording of a broadcast or cable programme of a designated class, or a copy of such a recording, may be made for the purpose of being placed in an archive maintained by a designated body without thereby infringing any copyright in the broadcast or cable programme or in any work included in it.

    (2) In subsection (1) 'designated' means designated for the purposes of this section by order of the Secretary of State, who shall not designate a body unless he is satisfied that it is not established or conducted for profit.

    (3) An order under this section shall be made by statutory instrument which shall be subject to annulment in pursuance of a resolution of either House of Parliament.

174. (1) The expression 'educational establishment' in a provision of this Part means:
    (a) any school, and
    (b) any other description of educational establishment specified for the purposes of this Part, or that provision, by order of the Secretary of State.

    (3) In subsection (1)(a) 'school':
    (a) in relation to England and Wales, has the same meaning as in the Education Act 1944;
    (b) in relation to Scotland, has the same meaning as in the Education (Scotland) Act 1962, except that it includes an approved school within the meaning of the Social Work (Scotland) Act 1968; and
    (c) in relation to Northern Ireland, has the same meaning as in the Education and Libraries (Northern Ireland) Order 1986.

Some definitions

175. (1) 'publication', in relation to a work:
    (a) means the issue of copies to the public, and
    (b) includes, in the case of a literary, dramatic or musical or artistic work, making it available to the public by means of an electronic retrieval system;
and related expressions shall be construed accordingly.

    (2) 'commercial publication', in relation to a literary, dramatic, musical or artistic work means:
    (a) issuing copies of the work to the public at a time when copies made in advance of the receipt of orders are generally available to the public, or

(b)   making the work available to the public by means of an electronic retrieval system;

and related expressions shall be construed accordingly.

(4)   The following do not constitute publication and references to commercial publication shall be construed accordingly:

(a)   in the case of a literary, dramatic or musical work:

(i)   the performance of the work, or

(ii)   the broadcasting of the work or its inclusion in a cable programme service (otherwise than for the purposes of an electronic retrieval system);

(b)   in the case of an artistic work:

(i)   the exhibition of the work,

(ii)   the issue to the public of copies of a graphic work representing, or of photographs of, a work of architecture in the form of a building or a model for a building, a sculpture or a work of artistic craftsman ship,

(iii)   the issue to the public of copies of a film including the work, or

(iv)   the broadcasting of the work or its inclusion in a cable programme service (otherwise than for the purposes of an electronic retrieval system);

(c)   in the case of a sound recording or film:

(i)   the work being played or shown in public, or

(ii)   the broadcasting of the work or its inclusion in a cable programme service.

Other definitions

178. In this Part:

'article', in the context of an article in a periodical, includes an item of any description.

'collective work' means:

(a)   a work of joint authorship, or

(b)   a work in which there are distinct contributions by different authors or in which works or parts of works of different authors are incorporated.

'computer-generated', in relation to a work, means that the work is generated by computer in circumstances such that there is no human author of the work;

'the Crown' includes the Crown in right of Her Majesty's Government in Northern Ireland or in any country outside the United Kingdom to which this Part extends;

'electronic' means actuated by electric, magnetic, electro-magnetic, electro-chemical or electro-mechanical energy, and 'in electronic form' means in a form usable only by electronic means;

'facsimile copy' includes a copy which is reduced or enlarged in scale;

'judicial proceedings' includes proceedings before any court, tribunal or person having authority to decide any matter affecting a person's legal rights or liabilities;

'parliamentary proceedings' includes proceedings of the Northern Ireland Assembly or of the European Parliament;

'rental' means any arrangement under which a copy of a work is made available;

(a)   for payment (in money or money's worth), or

(b)   in the course of a business, as part of services or amenities for which payment is made, on terms that it will or may be returned;

'reprographic copy' and 'reprographic copying' refer to copying by means of a reprographic process;

'reprographic process' means a process:

(a)   for making facsimile copies, or

(b)   involving the use of an appliance for making multiple copies, and includes, in relation to a work held in electronic form, any copying by electronic means, but does not include the making of a film or sound recording;

'sufficient acknowledgement' means an acknowledgement identifying the work in question by its title or other description, and identifying the author unless:

(a)   in the case of a published work, it is published anonymously,

(b)   in the case of an unpublished work, it is not possible for a person to ascertain the identity of the author by reasonable inquiry;

'typeface' includes an ornamental motif used in printing;

'unauthorised', as regards anything done in relation to a work, means done otherwise than:

(a)   by or with the licence of the copyright owner, or

(b)   if copyright does not subsist in the work, by or with the licence of the author or, in a case where section 11(2) would have applied, the author's employer or in either case, persons lawfully claiming under him, or

(c)   in pursuance of section 48 (copying, etc. of certain material by the Crown);

'writing' includes any form of notation or code, whether by hand or otherwise and regardless of the method by which, or medium in or on which, it is recorded, and 'written' shall be construed accordingly.

SI 89/1212   The Copyright (Librarians and Archivists) (Copying of copyright material) Regulations 1989

Descriptions of libraries and archives

3. (1) The descriptions of libraries specified in Part A of Schedule 1 to these Regulations are prescribed for the purposes of section 38 and 39 of the Act:

    Provided that any library conducted for profit shall not be a prescribed library for the purpose of those sections.

    (2) All libraries in the United Kingdom are prescribed for the purposes of sections 41, 42 and 43 of the Act as libraries the librarians of which may make and supply copies of any material to which those sections relate.

    (3) Any library of a description specified in Part A of Schedule 1 to these Regulations which is not conducted for profit and any library of the description specified in Part B of that Schedule which is not conducted for profit are prescribed for the purposes of Sections 41 and 42 of the Act as libraries for which copies of any material to which those sections relate may be made and supplied by the librarian of a prescribed library.

    (4) All archives in the United Kingdom are prescribed for the purposes of sections 42 and 43 of the Act as archives which may make and supply copies of any material to which those sections relate and any archive within the United Kingdom which is not conducted for profit is prescribed for the purposes of section 42 of the Act as an archive for which copies of any material to which that section relates may be made and supplied by the archivist of a prescribed archive.

    (5) In this regulation 'conducted for profit', in relation to a library or archive, means a library or archive which is established or conducted for profit or which forms part of, or is administered by, a body established or conducted for profit.

Copying by librarian of article or part of published work

4. (1) For the purposes of sections 38 and 39 of the Act the conditions specified in paragraph (2) of this regulation are prescribed as the conditions which must be complied with when the librarian of a prescribed library makes and supplies a copy of any article in a periodical or, as the case may be, of a part of a literary, dramatic or musical work from a published edition to a person requiring the copy.

(2) The prescribed conditions are:

    (a) that no copy of any article or any part of a work shall be supplied to the person requiring the same unless:

        (i) he satisfies the librarian that he requires the copy for purposes of research or private study and will not use it for any other purpose; and

        (ii) he has delivered to the librarian a declaration in writing, in relation to that article or part of a work, substantially in accordance with Form A in Schedule 2 to these Regulations and signed in the manner therein indicated;

    (b) that the librarian is satisfied that the requirement of such person and that of any other person:

        (i) are not similar, that is to say, the requirements are not for copies of substantially the same article or part of a work at substantially the same time and for substantially the same purpose; and

        (ii) are not related, that is to say, he and that person do not receive instruction to which the article or part of the work is relevant at the same time and place;

    (c) that such person is not furnished:

        (i) in the case of an article, with more than one copy of the article or more than one article contained in the same issue of a periodical; or

        (ii) in the case of a part of a published work, with more than one copy of the same material or with a copy of more than a reasonable proportion of any work; and

    (d) that such person is required to pay for the copy a sum not less than the cost (including a contribution to the general expenses of the library) attributable to its production.

(3) Unless the librarian is aware that the signed declaration delivered to him pursuant to paragraph (2)(a)(ii) above is false in a material particular, he may rely on it as to the matter he is required to be satisfied on under paragraph (2)(a)(i) above before making or supplying the copy.

Copying by librarian to supply other libraries

5. (1) For the purposes of section 41 of the Act the conditions specified in paragraph (2) of this regulation are prescribed as the conditions which must be complied with when the librarian of a prescribed

library makes and supplies to another prescribed library a copy of any article in a periodical or, as the case may be, of the whole or part of a published edition of a literary, dramatic or musical work required by that other prescribed library.

(2) The prescribed conditions are:

(a) that the other prescribed library is not furnished with more than one copy of the article or of the whole or part of the published edition; or

(b) that, where the requirement is for a copy of more than one article in the same issue of a periodical, or for a copy of the whole or part of a published edition, the other prescribed library furnishes a written statement to the effect that it is a prescribed library and that it does not know, and could not by reasonable inquiry ascertain, the name and address of a person entitled to authorise the making of the copy; and

(c) that the other prescribed library shall be required to pay for the copy a sum not less than the cost (including a contribution to the general expenses of the library) attributable to its production.

Copying by librarian or archivist for the purposes of replacing items in a permanent collection

6. (1) For the purposes of section 42 of the Act the conditions specified in paragraph (2) of this regulation are prescribed as the conditions which must be complied with before the librarian or, as the case may be, the archivist makes a copy from any item in the permanent collection of the library or archive in order to preserve or replace that item in the permanent collection of that library or archive or in the permanent collection of another prescribed library or archive.

(2) The prescribed conditions are:

(a) that the item in question is an item in the part of the permanent collection maintained by the library or archive wholly or mainly for the purposes of reference on the premises of the library or archive, or is an item in the permanent collection of the library or archive which is available on loan only to other libraries or archives;

(b) that it is not reasonably practicable for the librarian or archivist to purchase a copy of that item to fulfil the purpose under section 42(1)(a) or (b) of the Act;

101

(c) that the other prescribed library or archive furnishes a written statement to the effect that the item has been lost, destroyed or damaged and that it is not reasonably practicable for it to purchase a copy of that item, and that if a copy is supplied it will only be used to fulfil the purpose under section 42(1)(b) of the Act; and

(d) that the other prescribed library or archive shall be required to pay for the copy a sum not less than the cost (including a contribution to the general expenses of the library or archive) attributable to its production.

Copying by librarian or archivist of certain unpublished works

7. (1) For the purposes of section 43 of the Act the conditions specified in paragraph (2) of this regulation are prescribed as the conditions which must be complied with in the circumstances in which that section applies when the librarian or, as the case may be, the archivist makes and supplies a copy of the whole or part of a literary, dramatic or musical work from a document in the library or archive to a person requiring the copy.

(2) The prescribed conditions are:

(a) that no copy of the whole or part of the work shall be supplied to the person requiring the same unless:

(i) he satisfies the librarian or archivist that he requires the copy for purposes of research or private study and will not use it for any other purpose; and

(ii) he has delivered to the librarian or, as the case may be, the archivist, a declaration in writing, in relation to that work, substantially in accordance with Form B in Schedule 2 to these Regulations and signed in the manner therein indicated;

(b) that such person is not furnished with more than one copy of the same material; and

(c) that such person is required to pay for the copy a sum not less than the cost (including a contribution to the general expenses of the library or archive) attributable to its production.

(3) Unless the librarian or archivist is aware that the signed declaration delivered to him pursuant to paragraph (2)(a)(ii) above is false in a material particular, he may rely on it as to the matter he is required to be satisfied on under paragraph (2)(a)(i) above before making or supplying the copy.

SCHEDULE 1

PART A

1. Any library administered by:
   (a) a library authority within the meaning of the Public Libraries and Museums Act 1964 in relation to England and Wales;
   (b) a statutory library authority within the meaning of the Public Libraries (Scotland) Act 1955, in relation to Scotland;
   (c) an Education and Library Board within the meaning of the Education and Libraries (Northern Ireland) Order 1986, in relation to Northern Ireland.
2. The British Library, the National Library of Wales, the National Library of Scotland, the Bodleian Library, Oxford and the University Library, Cambridge.
3. Any library of a school within the meaning of section 174 of the Act and any library of a description of educational establishment specified under that section in the Copyright (Educational Establishments) (No 2) Order 1989.
4. Any parliamentary library or library administered as part of a government department, including a Northern Ireland department, or any library conducted for or administered by an agency which is administered by a Minister of the Crown.
5. Any library administered by:
   (a) In England and Wales, a local authority within the meaning of the Local Government Act 1972, the Common Council of the City of London or the Council of the Isles of Scilly;
   (b) In Scotland, a local authority within the meaning of the Local Government (Scotland) Act 1973;
   (c) In Northern Ireland, a district council established under the Local Government Act (Northern Ireland) 1972.
6. Any other library conducted for the purpose of facilitating or encouraging the study of bibliography, education, fine arts, history, languages, law, literature, medicine, music, philosophy, religion, science (including natural and social science) or technology, or administered by an establishment or organisation which is conducted wholly or mainly for such a purpose.

PART B

Any library outside the United Kingdom which is conducted wholly or mainly for the purpose of facilitating or encouraging the study of bibliography, education, fine arts, history, languages, law, literature, medicine, music, philosophy, religion, science (including natural and social science) or technology.

SCHEDULE 2

FORM A

DECLARATION: COPY OF ARTICLE OR PART OF PUBLISHED WORK

To:

The Librarian of ....Library
(Address of Library)

Please supply me with a copy of:
* the article in the periodical, the particulars of which are
  [   ]
* the part of the published work, the particulars of which are
  [   ]
required by me for the purposes of research or private study.

2. I declare that:
   (a) I have not previously been supplied with a copy of the same material by you or any other librarian;
   (b) I will not use the copy except for research or private study and will not supply a copy of it to any other person; and
   (c) to the best of my knowledge no other person with whom I work or study has made or intends to make, at or about the same time as this request, a request for substantially the same material for substantially the same purpose.

3. I understand that if the declaration is false in a material particular the copy supplied to me by you will be an infringing copy and that I shall be liable for infringement of copyright as if I had made the copy myself.

                           **Signature.....................
                               Date ....
Name ....
Address ....

* Delete whichever is inappropriate.
** This must be the personal signature of the person making the request. A stamped or typewritten signature, or the signature of an agent, is NOT acceptable.

FORM B

DECLARATION: COPY OF WHOLE OR PART OF UNPUBLISHED WORK

To:

The *Librarian/Archivist of .... *Library/Archive
(Address of Library/Archive)

Please supply me with a copy of:
the *whole/following part [particulars of part] of the [particulars of
the unpublished work] required by me for the purposes of research
or private study.

2. I declare that:
   (a) I have not previously been supplied with a copy of the same
       material by you or any other librarian or archivist;
   (b) I will not use the copy except for research or private study and
       will not supply a copy of it to any other person; and
   (c) to the best of my knowledge the work had not been published
       before the document was deposited in your *library/archive and
       the copyright owner has not prohibited copying of the work.

3. I understand that if the declaration is false in a material particular
   the copy supplied to me by you will be an infringing copy and that
   I shall be liable for infringement of copyright as if I had made the
   copy myself.

                              **Signature......................
                                  Date.........................

Name...
Address..

* Delete whichever is inappropriate.
** This must be the personal signature of the person making the request.
   A stamped or typewritten signature, or the signature of an agent,
   is NOT acceptable.

SI 89/1068 Copyright (Educational Establishments) (No 2) Order 1989

The descriptions of educational establishments mentioned in the Schedule to this Order are specified for the purposes of Part I of the Act.

SCHEDULE

1. Any university empowered by Royal Charter or Act of Parliament to award degrees and any college, or institution in the nature of a college, in such a university.
2. Any institution providing further education within the meaning of section 1(5)(b) of the Education (Scotland) Act 1980 and any educational establishment (other than a school) within the meaning of section 135(1) of that Act.
3. Any institution providing further education within the meaning of article 5(c) of the Education and Libraries (Northern Ireland) Order 1986 and any college of education within the meaning of that Order.
4. Any institution the sole or main purpose of which is to provide further education within the meaning of section 41 of the Education Act 1944 or higher education within the meaning of section 120 of the Education Reform Act 1988, or both.

Index

110

obsolescence 246, 337, 376
OHP 76, 284, 295, 323
open to the public, definition 293
Optical Character Recognition 70
optical disc 371*a*
oral history 333, 345, 347
organization, as author 39
  see also anonymous works
Organisation of American States
  68
overhead transparencies *see* OHP
owner, ownership 13-15
  definition 26-31
  copying 69-70
  issuing copies 78-80
  performance 81-86
  broadcasting 87
  adaptation 88-95
  translation 88
  databases 114

paintings *see* artistic works
Parliamentary copyright 65-68
  qualification of authorship 7
Parliamentary libraries 203
Parliamentary proceedings 259-260
payment
  for copying in libraries 161,
    167-8, 188-9, 192-4
  for copying unpublished works
    253
  Copyright Clearance Center 409
  interlibrary copying 213, 223,
    225
  preservation 238
  rental right 340, 379
  archival folksong recordings
    361
performance 25*a*, 57, 81-6, 333,
    343-4, 347, 349, 381, 387, 402
  Peter Pan 8
  examination 125
periodicals
  ownership of copyright 40
  duration 50-51
  limits on copying 135-143
  definition 144
  subscription rates 145
  single article 154
  copying 161, 171

interlibrary copying 213
  and illustrations 138, 329
  abstracts 146
  Copyright Clearance Center 409
permanent collection, definition
    236, 239, 241
permanent public display 292-3
perpetual copyright 8, 288, 291
Peter Pan 8
photographs
  current events 117-8, 312
  criticism or review 314
  duration of copyright 288
  educational copying 320
  as advertisement 315-6
  library copying 326
  as artistic works 282*a*
  of artistic works 292, 294, 299,
    309
  accompanying article 138, 329
  books mostly made up of 160
  incidental inclusion in 298
  of films 398*a*
pictures − as adaptation 90-1, 296
plans *see* artistic works
playing a work *see* performing
plays 8, 25*a*, 83, 86, 88
poems 81, 83-4, 116
pottery *see* artistic works
prescribed archives, definition 235
prescribed libraries, definition
    203ff
preservation, copying for 234-242
  artistic works 331
  sound recordings 356
private libraries 211
private study 103-4, 106, 122, 161
  see also research and fair dealing
prohibited copying 77, 246, 248-9
pseudonymous works 36
  see also anonymous works
public administration 259-271, 371
public exhibition 291
public inspection 261-271
  unpublished material 53, 55
  artistic works 331
  sound recordings 370
Public Lending Right 343, 417
  see also list of addresses
public libraries

112

113

18.00